"For nearly five decades I've been privileged to witness Ron Sider's groundbreaking work as a leading evangelical voice for the imperatives of social justice. His earned reputation is as compelling Christian author and energetic social activist. But I welcome the publication of *Preaching the Gospel* because we see the whole of Ron's ministry and commitment. These sermons and lectures reflect on marriage and holiness, as well as apartheid and violence. He ponders baptism and communion, as well as justice and peacemaking. This book is a treasure of Ron Sider's pastoral and prophetic wisdom, held together holistically, just as he has lived. It's a gift to all who have been inspired by his faithful witness."

—**Wesley Granberg-Michaelson**, author of *Without Oars: Casting Off into a Life of Pilgrimage* and General Secretary Emeritus, Reformed Church in America

"I have heard Ron Sider preach over the past forty-five years. His sermons and prophetic speeches were a fountain of 'understanding the times,' anointed by the Holy Spirit, wrapped in a biblical and historical foundation that flowed like a river to one's soul. What an incredible gift to now have these sermons and prophetic speeches available for these days and new generations to come. They are ageless."

—**Jo Anne Lyon**, General Superintendent Emerita of the Wesleyan Church

"Ron Sider is one of the most powerful and prophetic voices in Christianity, yet his heart is deeply empathetic and his stories are as winsome as they are insightful. This book is where holiness and humility, justice and tenderness, reproach and repentance become partners."

—**Joel C. Hunter**, former senior pastor of Northland Church, and chairman of Community Resource Network

"Perhaps the closest thing we have to a pastoral epistle in our time is a sermon manuscript—and the closest thing to a modern apostle is a preacher whose ministry extends beyond the local congregation. In this collection of inspiring and instructive sermons delivered in many places over a decades-long global ministry, the venerable Dr. Ronald Sider becomes a kind of contemporary St. Paul. This volume will be a precious resource for a long time to come."

—**Rob Schenck**, president of The Dietrich Bonhoeffer Institute, Washington, DC

"This book is a beautiful collection of some of Ron's most powerful, edifying, and deeply personal sermons. In *Preaching the Gospel*, Ron does just that, and is all the more effective by drawing upon some of the most important milestones in his and his family's life. His commitment to Jesus and justice shine through. I highly commend this book for your consideration."

—**Adam Russell Taylor**, president of Sojourners and author of *A More Perfect Union: A New Vision for Building the Beloved Community*

Preaching the Gospel

Preaching the Gospel

Collected Sermons on Discipleship, Mission,
Peace, Justice, and the Sacraments

Ronald J. Sider

CASCADE *Books* · Eugene, Oregon

PREACHING THE GOSPEL
Collected Sermons on Discipleship, Mission, Peace, Justice,
and the Sacraments

Cascade Books
An Imprint of Wipf and Stock Publishers
199 W. 8th Ave., Suite 3
Eugene, OR 97401

www.wipfandstock.com

PAPERBACK ISBN: 978-1-7252-8601-6
HARDCOVER ISBN: 978-1-7252-8600-9
EBOOK ISBN: 978-1-7252-8602-3

Cataloguing-in-Publication data:

Names: Sider, Ronald J., author.

Title: Preaching the gospel : collected sermons on discipleship, mission,
peace, justice, and the sacraments / by Ronald J. Sider.

Description: Eugene, OR: Cascade Books, 2021.

Identifiers: ISBN 978-1-7252-8601-6 (paperback) | ISBN 978-1-7252-
8600-9 (hardcover) | ISBN 978-1-7252-8602-3 (ebook)

Subjects: LCSH: Ronald J. Sider, 1931–. | Sermons.

Classification: BT7364.4 .S55 2021 (print) | BT7364 (ebook)

Manufactured in the U.S.A.   06/18/21

Contents

PART ONE: Following Jesus in Faithful Discipleship

Chapter 1: "I Will Meet You on the Other Side, Dad"

[The sermon I preached at the funeral of my Dad (Rev. James P. Sider) on January 4, 2004, at Rosebank Brethren in Christ Church in Rosebank, Ontario, Canada.]

THIS WEDNESDAY, IMMEDIATELY AFTER listening to the voice messages that Dad had died, I dropped to my knees to thank God for this wonderful man. I felt overwhelmed with gratitude that this loving father, caring husband, successful farmer, and pastor had been my father. Muriel, Miriam, Lucille, Tennyson, and I all feel, as Tennyson said in the tribute, that we have been incredibly blessed, way beyond measure, to have this very good man and his darling wife our mother as our parents. They loved each other dearly. They loved each of us deeply, warmly, and abundantly. And above all they loved their Lord—and thus gave us the most precious gift parents can bestow—a happy, loving, encouraging home centered on Christ.

The tribute that Tennyson gave offered many examples of how special Dad was. Let me share just two more stories.

When Dad was about forty-nine, he had an operation to remove one of his kidneys. After the operation, the surgeon came to talk to Dad. He said: "There is good news and bad news. The good news is you do not have cancer. The bad news is that I accidentally damaged another organ close to your kidney. It won't be life threatening, but may cause some problems."

Twenty-five or so years later, Dad told this story to his current doctor. That doctor's immediate response was: "Did you sue him?" "Did I sue him?" Dad asked, puzzled. "Of course not. He was doing his best and then he came and told me what happened. Of course I didn't sue him."

The second story comes from the last few years when Dad reluctantly had to accept more and more help for daily living. But he showed amazing kindness and appreciation for his nurses and aides, regularly thanking them for all their loving care. One day somebody—I don't remember that Dad ever told me who it was—said something pretty nasty to Dad.

Almost instantly, before Dad responded to the person, a Scripture and a memory from childhood popped into Dad's head. He remembered a time when he was a boy attending a church meeting. Two men got into a vigorous quarrel and stepped outside to settle the matter. Dad sneaked out to watch the fight. But a third man came out and quoted Psalm 119:165: "Great peace have they which love the law; and nothing shall offend them." And the quarrel ended.

Dad told us that he had not thought of that incident or Scripture for decades. But God reminded him of it just when he needed help to respond kindly to a nasty, hurtful comment. I won't, but I could go on telling story after story to demonstrate what a special, wonderful man Dad was.

One of the great honors and privileges of my life was to have Dad ask me a year or so ago to preach his funeral sermon.

Just five days before Dad died, as I was driving from Windsor to Cambridge to see my Dad for the last time, another set of thoughts rippled through my mind. Yes, Dad was a wonderful man and he blessed thousands of people through his ministry. But he was just one of over six billion people living on a tiny fragile planet in a small solar system in one little corner of the Milky Way, which is just one vast galaxy with billions of stars in an almost incomprehensibly huge universe with 120 billion galaxies, each of which has billions of stars like our sun. Dad's ninety years of life was just a momentary flicker of time in this vast system that has been changing and growing for billions of years. And in that flicker of time—those ninety years of good life that appeared for an instant and then disappeared again—in that flicker of time, Dad did not significantly change politics, science, or even the church. Dad appeared for an instant or two and then was gone again.

So what meaning does his life have now? I know what Dad's answer would be. And I agree completely with him.

Dad knew that this vast, complex universe that scientists are increasingly beginning to understand—this whole vast universe came from the loving hand of an all-wise God. This personal God gently shaped our gorgeous, almost infinitely intricate world, and then made human beings in God's very own image and called them to be God's stewards, to trace God's stupendous design in every corner of the world. God even invited them to join the Almighty Creator as little creators developing fruitful farms, nurturing loving families, and shaping complex civilizations.

Tragically, God's human stewards messed everything up. Instead of worshipping and obeying God and submitting to the moral order God built into the world, we proudly decided to pretend that we are God. We chose to make our own rules. We worshipped the creation rather than the Creator. The result is pain, brokenness, evil, tragedy everywhere—broken families, unfaithfulness, heartbreak, crime, war, savagery, and destruction wherever we look.

But Dad knew that God refused to abandon the world God loved, even when we stubbornly rejected God and ravaged our neighbors. God began to speak in a special way to an Iraqi named Abram and his children. God sent mighty leaders and faithful prophets to show Abraham's children how to live in peace, justice, and wholeness. But after brief periods of obedience and prosperity, they always rejected God's way and created more brokenness and agony.

Finally, Dad knew, the Creator of 120 billion spinning galaxies decided to come himself to this little planet to show us the way and offer a path out of our tragedy and brokenness. The Creator of the universe became a vulnerable embryo, a little speck of matter in the womb of a teenage Jewish virgin. In obedient faith, this trembling maiden responded to God's utterly astounding act, welcoming the God of the universe who became human flesh and blood in her nine months of pregnancy. And when she and her husband Joseph could find no place in the inn, she gave birth to the Creator of the universe in a barn and called him Jesus, Savior, as the angel had instructed.

For most of his life, Jesus was an obedient son, learning from Joseph how to be a gifted carpenter. Visibly, this young man cutting and sanding tables and chairs was just another Galilean craftsman. But in truth he was also the Creator of the galaxies, teaching us by his physical labor the goodness and beauty of the material world, of everyday work and ordinary family life.

At about thirty, this young carpenter became a strange kind of wandering preacher and successful teacher. He healed the sick, cared especially about the poor, and welcomed dispossessed, marginalized folk like women and lepers. And he began to challenge the status quo in all kinds of ways—its attitude toward the poor, the sick, women, war and violence.

He also claimed to be the long expected Jewish Messiah. For many centuries, Jewish prophets had promised that sometime in the future, a descendant of King David would come to forgive sin in a new way, to write God's law on people's hearts, and to bring peace and justice to the whole world. Secretly at first, and then more and more openly, Jesus claimed to be that long-expected Messiah. Slowly, too, he made even more stunning claims—to have divine authority to forgive sins, to be Lord of the Sabbath, even to be the very Son of God. So the Jewish and Roman authorities collaborated to kill him as a dangerous social radical and a heretical blasphemer. They crucified him assuming that would squelch his threatening ideas forever.

But three days later, Jesus burst from the tomb and appeared to his astonished disciples, demonstrating by his bodily resurrection that death had been conquered for all who would believe. And he taught them that his death on the cross offered total, unconditional divine forgiveness for all who would humbly recognize their sin and ask God to wipe it away. And the risen Lord promised to return some day to complete his victory over every evil, brokenness, sin, and injustice, and complete the restoration of the entire creation to wholeness.

This true, utterly astounding, story—that the Creator of the universe actually lived on this earth once, died for our sins once for all and rose bodily from the dead to offer life forever with God to all who believe, and promised to return to earth some day to fully renew the whole creation—this story spread like wildfire. Within three short centuries, it conquered the most powerful pagan empire of human history. Century after century, more and more broken people, no matter how messed up their lives, found liberating forgiveness and new, transformed life in this wondrous story so that by the time Dad ended his ministry as a preacher of this glorious story, over two billion people in every country on earth were followers of this amazing carpenter.

Dad knew that his life had meaning—wonderful, powerful meaning—because he was a part, even though just a small part, of this glorious story. Dad knew that in every act of kindness to friend and neighbor, he was responding obediently to the way the Creator made the world and was joining the Creator's grand design for the universe. In all Dad's activity as a faithful farmer—growing good crops of corn, wheat, oats, and red clover, developing a great herd of registered Holstein cows—Dad was fulfilling the Creator's mandate to care for the creation and create new things. In all Dad's activity as a loving husband—delighting in and ever learning more about serving his darling wife of fifty-nine years—Dad gave his children and the world an attractive picture of the wondrous goodness and joy of faithful marriage. In all Dad's activity as a wonderful father—loving each child uniquely, setting clear, firm family rules, slowly allowing each maturing child to make their own decisions even when he and Mom disagreed, continuing to love and support us even when we stumbled and fell—Dad and Mom offered a tremendous model of excellent parenting. In all Dad's activity as a church leader—teaching biblical truth, preaching revival services, inviting people to personal faith in the Savior, counseling and encouraging struggling church members—Dad was playing his small part in nurturing that ever-growing circle of two billion-plus disciples of Christ his Lord.

In every sector of Dad's life—his farming, his family, his ministry—Dad's seemingly insignificant daily activities were a part of God's glorious divine plan of creating a stupendously beautiful, complex world and restoring everything in that world to the wholeness the Creator placed here at the beginning. In joining and playing his part in that grand design, Dad found strong meaning and powerful joy that lasted for a lifetime.

And from the Author of that grand design, Dad also found the strength to live the way he knew the Creator made us to live. Satan tempts all of us to selfishness, to temporary thrills that soon sour and turn to bitterness and pain. Dad discovered that the same Almighty God who raised his Lord Jesus from the dead was now at work in his personal life raising him to a new life of increasing unselfishness and growing kindness, providing the daily strength to live with integrity, love, and faithfulness.

I know that if Dad were alive and with us this afternoon, there is just one thing he would want to add. And that is the amazing truth that the loving Creator of the universe continues to gently invite every person here, indeed every person on planet earth, to join God's grand plan and find meaning, healing, and joy in this glorious story.

We don't have to be famous to play an important role in God's grand design. Every single one of us, as we are good children, faithful parents, and loving grandparents—as we change diapers, kiss away children's tears, work faithfully to provide for our family—in those acts, every one of us brings joy to the Creator.

Every single one of us as we are faithful to our calling—as electricians, secretaries, artists, teachers, scientists, philosophers, plumbers, farmers, pastors, tour guides—serve our neighbors in all these acts and make our small contribution to the kind of wholesome civilization that the Creator intends.

Every single one of us as we are active in Christian ministry, whether in the local congregation or beyond—as faithful church attendee, Sunday School teacher, bookkeeper, usher, pastor, national board member, missionary, evangelist, mentor of youth—in all these activities we play our own crucial part in God's grand design, helping more and more persons find their place in Jesus' wondrous story.

Dad often said that nothing, absolutely nothing, matters as much as embracing Jesus' astounding story. Dad knew that was true both for this life and for all eternity. Over his ninety years on this earth, Dad discovered in his own personal experience that submitting to God's way and living within God's grand design is the best way to happiness, meaning, and joy—now in this life. And now, as he stands on the other shore in the very presence of the risen Lord Jesus, Dad knows with a clarity we cannot have here that Jesus' wondrous story is the way to joy unspeakable, not just for this life but for all eternity. Dad would not want me to end without reminding us all of the blessed simplicity of embracing this wondrous story.

Jesus promised: "For God so loved the world that he gave his one and only Son, that whoever believes in him shall not perish but have eternal life."

That is the divine offer to every one of us today—those who embraced this promise many decades ago, those who came to rejoice in this truth much more recently, those who may just now surrender their hearts and welcome this truth as the center of their life.

In the last few years, as Dad's longing to go home grew ever stronger, I prayed with him many times that God would take him soon. And I promised him as I promised Mother, that I would, by God's good grace, meet them on the other shore. They stand together now on the other side with arms outstretched, inviting each one of us here today to promise the same: Dad, Grandpa, friend, pastor, I'll meet you on the other side.

So help us God, Amen.

Chapter 2: **Putting the Kingdom First**

[The commencement address I gave on June 7, 1986, at the graduation of my son, Michael Jay Sider, from Christopher Dock Mennonite High School in Lansdale, Pennsylvania. In the next fifteen years, I used it in sermons to youth groups in the United States and Canada.]

I FELT VERY HONORED to be asked to speak tonight. But then last night at the Baccalaureate Service, a student came up to me and said: "Wow, they must have been scraping the bottom of the barrel if the only person they could get to speak was a parent." Seriously, however, speaking at the graduation of a son is a very special privilege and I do very sincerely want to thank the senior class and the administration for this special joy.

But it is also rather scary. To make sure I would not blow it too badly, I decided to seek advice from a number of Christopher Dock seniors who happened to find their way to our home for a party after getting lost in Philadelphia. (No, don't look at me that way. I promised I would not tell your moms and dads the details.) I asked them what I should say. Nobody would help me. Actually, one did. My son Michael gave me quite a bit of advice. But I decided to ignore that—at least partially. So don't blame him.

One parent also passed along a bit of wisdom. She said the most important aspect of my address for the seniors would be when I stopped. You can decide later on whether I ignored that wonderful commentary on her expectations for my address.

Thinking as a parent about this celebration of transition from high school to adult life raised a very basic question for me. What do I really want in life for Michael? What do each of you parents here today most want for your graduating son or daughter?

I think I can summarize it all in one word: happiness. For Michael and every one of you graduates, I wish happiness. This little planet is a fantastic place full of incredible surprise and splendor. I hope you can rejoice in its goodness and beauty through travel, artistic expression, and meaningful employment. I hope you enjoy the happiness of material comfort and the peace and security of never having to face the ravages of disease, famine, and war. For each of you seniors, I pray for that happiness that comes from experiencing the material goodness of creation.

But there is something I want far, far more for each of you than material well-being. I long for each of you the joy and happiness of Christian family. For those of you who choose to marry, I wish you the happiness of a Christian marriage that lasts for a lifetime of ecstasy and pain, failure and growth, and steady progress in commitment and love. If I had to choose, I would choose a lifetime of poverty rather than the agony of brokenness and divorce in marriage.

Lifelong commitment in Christian marriage is not all lollipops and emotional highs. In the best of marriages there is struggle, pain, and failure. But lifelong marriage in Christ is a priceless gift of beauty, security, and joy. I wish each of you the happiness of Christian family.

Then there is one more thing. It is infinitely more precious than everything else I have talked about. It is the happiness of a living personal relationship with the Creator of the galaxies. That is the pearl of great price for which I would be willing to surrender all the other joys I have mentioned—wife, family, material well-being, even physical life itself.

All those other forms of happiness are good. They are gifts from God. But they are finite, limited, partial. You and I are made to find ultimate meaning and happiness only as we walk humbly and obediently with our Almighty Father. You and I are made to live forever in the presence of the Lord of the Universe. The joy of that relationship far exceeds every earthly happiness.

That's why Jesus said: "Seek first his kingdom and his righteousness and all these things will be given to you as well" (Matthew 6:33).

I want to stress three important things that follow from this text.

The first is a paradox. You cannot get happiness by aiming at it. It comes only as a by-product when you aim at something else. If you aim at material happiness and make wealth your idol, you will get the gnawing emptiness of the rich person who constantly tears down and builds new barns in an ever more frantic search for security and satisfaction in things. If you aim at sexual happiness and make sexual thrills your idol, you will get loneliness, divorce, the suicide of a Marilyn Monroe, or the death by AIDS of a Rock Hudson.

Graham Kerr is a friend who formerly sought happiness in possessions, fame, and adulterous thrills. He became the host of an internationally famous TV program called *The Galloping Gourmet*. At the peak of his success, his TV program was the most widely watched program in history. And Graham had all the happiness that a millionaire's money could buy—fancy cars, splendid houses, wine, women, and song. And he was miserable. At the height of all this so-called "happiness," Graham's life was a shambles. He was an alcoholic and his marriage was a disaster.

Then one day a maid in their home said to his wife, Treena, "I know what could change your life. Come to church with me on Sunday." Treena was desperate so she went. That Sunday morning, she met Christ and her life was transformed. Graham was not interested in his wife's new religious ideas at first. But he watched her new behavior and joy. Three months later, he decided that whatever had happened to Treena was good enough for him. He, too, accepted Christ as Lord and Savior. No longer did Graham aim at happiness through fame, money, and sex. Since then, Graham and Treena's lives have been radically changed. Christ and his kingdom came first. Graham stopped his TV program. They gave away their millions. They now live a simple lifestyle and serve in a Christian ministry that combines evangelism and agricultural development.

They don't have many of the things they used to have, although they still have enough. But you only need to spend a little time with them to see a fantastic joy in their marriage. And together they have an excitement in Christian ministry to the poor that transcends the thrill of top ratings for TV audiences.

Graham and Treena have truly put the kingdom first in their lives. Christ is Lord and therefore they seek to live all the righteousness of family life, justice, and care for the poor that God desires. By aiming at the kingdom and its righteousness, they have also found happiness as a by-product—the deep, abiding happiness of a dynamic walk with God; the secure happiness of Christian marriage; and the happiness that comes from having enough of all the good gifts of the earth.

Putting the kingdom first also puts everything else in just the right place. The Almighty Designer knows how everything fits together. So if we follow God's way for our lives, then we get everything right—both our relationship with God and with neighbor and the earth. That's why Jesus said that if we seek first the kingdom, then we will have everything else we need as a by-product.

St. Augustine said that all of creation is a ring from our Beloved. Material things are like a wonderful, special ring given to you and me by our divine Lover, God Almighty.

God wants us to enjoy them. But we must never forget the Beloved who gave them. If your fiance gives you a special ring, he wants you to enjoy it. But think of how silly it would be to forget your fiance and think only of the ring. In fact if we concentrate all our attention on the gift and forget the Giver, then we lose even the happiness God wants us to receive from the gift. It is only when we put God first, only when we do not look first of all for happiness through created things, that we get even that happiness as a by-product.

Don't let anybody ever tell you that God does not want you and me to enjoy happiness. God wants you to dance with joy over the happiness of a loving family, a fulfilling job, a good house, enough food and money for daily needs and some left over for grand celebration of special occasions like graduation from high school.

God would not have filled every little nook and cranny of creation with such gorgeous color and surprising splendor if God had not intended you and me to discover happiness in earthly things. But you cannot find happiness if you aim at it directly.

It comes as a by-product when you put God's kingdom first.

Jesus' promise that earthly happiness comes as a by-product if we put the kingdom first does not mean we will never have trouble, danger, and struggle. Satan stalks the earth, seeking to destroy all the goodness God has created. Putting the kingdom first means defying Satan and all who obey him. And that can be costly. But even then, there is a deep abiding happiness in following Christ even at the toughest times.

I have an Uncle Walter Winger—one of those Wingers whose Mennonite ancestors may go back to sixteenth-century Swiss Mennonites in the Alps. Back then, when they put the kingdom first, they got hunted like animals, drowned in the rivers, and burned at the stake.

My Uncle Walter was one of the early missionaries to Africa.

That was a tough, painful, lonely calling. But he rejoiced in the ministry God had given him. I remember him as an old man full of energy and the joy of God. And do you know what his favorite biblical text was? Matthew 6:33: "Seek first his kingdom and his righteousness and all these things will be given to you as well." He quoted Matthew 6:33 so often with so much trust in its truth that even today years later, I still think of Matthew 6:33 as Uncle Walter's verse.

Kevin King is a young friend and Mennonite farm boy who has put the kingdom first. He has told me that he would like to raise a family on a Pennsylvania farm. But for awhile, God called him to be a volunteer with Mennonite Central Committee (MCC) in Brazil. So he has lived in a desperately poor village in the poorest section of northeast Brazil, helping malnourished peasants learn how to build a dam and grow better corn. I have an MCC poster on my wall that pictures Kevin and a poor Brazilian farmer looking proudly at that first tall crop of corn. There is a quiet happiness in Kevin's face that proves that even when putting the kingdom first means lonely separation from family, risk of tropical disease, and living on thirty-five dollars a month, even then Jesus' promise is still true. When we put the kingdom first, we get wonderful, deep, abiding happiness as a by-product. That is my first point.

There is a second important truth that comes from Jesus' teaching about the kingdom. Jesus' kingdom challenges the status quo—the status quo is just a fancy term for talking about the sad mess all around us—Jesus' kingdom challenges the status quo at every point that it is wrong.

Jesus must have infuriated the men of his day. They were happy with the easy divorce laws that allowed them to get rid of their wives on almost any pretext. Jesus said no. He said God's way, the kingdom way, is for one man and one woman to live in life-long covenant. Men of Jesus' day were also very prejudiced against women and considered them inferior. Men thought it was a disgrace to appear in public with women. They said it was better to burn a copy of the Old Testament than give it to a woman. There was even a prayer that Jewish males of Jesus' day prayed that said: "I thank God I am not a Gentile, a slave, or a woman." Jesus said no. He totally rejected that male prejudice. He appeared with women in public. He discussed theology with them. He honored them with the first resurrection appearance even though the testimony of a woman had no weight in court. Jesus said God's way, the kingdom's way, is equal dignity and respect for all. Jesus also upset the rulers of his day. They loved to lord it over their subjects and pretend that it was for the good of everyone. Jesus said no. He said leaders should be servants if they want to follow kingdom values.

And Jesus terrified the economic establishment. He was constantly talking about sharing with the poor. He insisted that we should loan to the poor even if there is no hope of repayment. And as if that was not enough, he said that those who do not feed the hungry and clothe the naked go to hell. God's way, the kingdom's way, includes a costly concern for the poor and the weak.

Perhaps most radical of all, Jesus said the normal human way of security through violence is wrong. Humanity has always sought peace and justice through the sword. Jesus said no. He called on his followers to love even their enemies and show the world the kingdom's new way to peace.

Well, you can see why Jesus was not too popular with the supporters of the status quo. The values of Jesus' kingdom challenged the status quo so sharply that they had to change the way they lived or get rid of Jesus. They chose to kill him rather than put the kingdom first.

You know, seniors, Jesus' kingdom still challenges our world today in the same pointed way. Our world is crazy, even though it often looks enticing in the fast track.

Think of family life. Instead of being the centers of love and security God intended, our homes are often hell on earth. Half of our marriages dissolve in divorce. Millions of kids watch their parents fight and feud, ripping each other and their families to shreds.

Lancaster Mennonite High School's chorus sang at our church a few weeks ago. One song was a beautiful piece written by their director, Clyde Hollinger. It is called "You Don't Have to Fear the Storm." He wrote it for his little son who was terrified one stormy summer evening by the crack and roar of thunder. In the song, Clyde tells how he took his little boy in his arms, held him real tight, and said softly, "Son, you don't have to fear the storm. I will be here with you all the time; you can trust my word."

You know, seniors, half the fathers and mothers today cannot honestly sing that song. You cannot honestly promise always to be there if as so many parents do, you are going to end your marriage covenant and seek divorce when the going gets tough.

I want to ask each of you seniors a question. Do you believe Jesus knew what he was talking about? Do you intend to put his kingdom values first in your life? If you do, then you are going to have to look this crazy society straight in the eye and say: "NO! NO! I refuse your crazy sexual values. I will wait till marriage. I will be faithful to my spouse. I will make a marriage promise before God Almighty that I will keep all my life for better or for worse, in pain and in joy." I can promise you that will sometimes be tough. I can promise you that living that kingdom way will require a stubborn determination to defy the status quo that Hollywood makes so attractive. And I can also promise you—on the authority of the One who sculptured the Rocky Mountains and set the stars in place—that the kingdom's way on marriage is the way to deep, abiding, lifelong happiness.

Jesus' kingdom challenges the economic status quo in exactly the same way. More and more today, our society says that happiness comes from money and big houses, limousines and luxuries that wealth can purchase. Our brightest and best go for the big money that buys trendy vacations, fashionable clothes, and meals at the best restaurants.

And you know more and more of us Mennonites are buying that vision of the good life, that road to happiness. Is that really what you seniors want to do with your lives? Do you want to devote the best years of your life to worshipping expensive gadgets, costly perfumes, and ever more luxurious things, at a time when millions starve and billions have never once heard the Good News of Jesus' love for them?

I ask you graduating seniors: Do you really believe Jesus? Do you believe what he said about sharing your lives with the poor? Will you build bigger and bigger barns for yourself while Lazarus starves at the door?

I beg you to put the kingdom first. I beg you to join Kevin and hundreds of other MCC volunteers linking arms with the poor in Brazil and Bangladesh, Peru and the Philippines. I beg you to join the brave band of my Uncle Walter and the hundreds of thousands of others who have left comfort and security to tell a dying world of the love of Jesus. I beg you to stay here in Lansdale or Philadelphia or Souderton and create successful farms, professional careers, and productive businesses whose daily practices and financial resources are totally surrendered to Christ and the work of his kingdom.

If you put the kingdom first in this area of your life, you will have to defy the status quo as surely as in the area of sex and marriage. And it will often be tough and costly. But here, too, I can promise you—on the authority of the One who created all the wealth of our fabulous planet and billions of others as well—that putting the kingdom first in your economic choices is the way to abiding happiness. It is the way to a God-given happiness that the richest Rockefeller never knows. But Mother Teresa, Uncle Walter, and Kevin King enjoy it all the time.

Thus far we have thought together about the way happiness comes as a by-product when we put the kingdom first. And we have also seen how Jesus' kingdom radically challenges the way our fallen, sinful world lives.

I have a third point—since every good speech must have three points. But this is my last and briefest comment. I think this generation of Mennonites, if we put the kingdom first, has an unusual opportunity to take the values of Jesus' kingdom into every corner of modern life.

You know, until fairly recently, we misunderstood separation from the world in a way that put up big barriers between ourselves and the rest of society. We misunderstood separation as withdrawal from the world rather than separation from the sin of the world. And so we withdrew to the countryside, wore our plain clothes and had little to do with others except as that was necessary to be successful farmers. So there was not too much opportunity to share Jesus' kingdom values with other people.

You young people don't really know too much about all that because the big changes happened just before you arrived on the scene. When I finished grade eight, I still parted my hair in the middle and I never wore a necktie. And I think my Amish wife must have been born with long pigtails and a covering. I'll never forget the agony I went through in my first few weeks of high school at Niagara Christian College, a Brethren in Christ high school much like Christopher Dock. I always parted my hair in the middle, but that summer before grade nine I got a brush cut. As my hair grew longer, I wanted desperately to part my hair on the side. But I thought that might be sinful. So I prayed and struggled and kept combing it straight forward in order to postpone the final hour of decision. Finally, after far more anguish than you can imagine, I combed it to the side. One big step for Ron Sider. One small step for correcting our misunderstanding that separation from the sin of the world means cultural withdrawal and living last century's styles.

But all that has changed. And that means this generation of Mennonites face fantastic new opportunity. And also a new danger.

We are no longer primarily farmers. We are doctors and dentists, carpenters and plumbers, business leaders and professors, politicians and artists. Unlike Mennonites for hundreds of years, this generation, your generation, seniors, is at the heart of our society in a new, exciting way. You have a historic opportunity to take the vision of Jesus' kingdom and apply it in the world of business and art, music and law, drama and medicine.

This world is God's world even though sin has blown through God's good creation like a raging hurricane. God is about the business of restoring the broken beauty of creation to the glory and wholeness God originally intended. That's what the Good News of the kingdom is all about. Christians believe that in spite of the power of evil all around, it is possible now by God's grace to reject adultery and live the kingdom teaching in lifelong marriage; it is possible now to reject war and live the kingdom's way of reconciliation and peace; it is possible now to run our businesses honestly and justly and share with the poor the way Jesus did. It is possible now to reject the brokenness of modern filmmaking, art, music, law, and medicine and do all those things in a way that shouts to the world that the way of the kingdom is a better way.

I hope you seniors will rise to this fantastic opportunity.

I expect to meet you in twenty-five years transforming American education, health care, law, culture, and, yes, even politics, so that all those areas of society look a little more like the kingdom Jesus announced.

But notice the new danger that accompanies this new opportunity. Our great temptation is no longer withdrawal from the world. Our greatest temptation today is conformity to the sin of society. As you and I plunge into the center of modern life, we experience powerful, demonic temptations to do things the way Hollywood and Wall Street and the Pentagon do things rather than the way Jesus does.

The strange thing is that only if we cling firmly to a biblical understanding of separation from the world's sin, only then can we make a difference as we plunge into the center of modern society. The last thing our sad world needs is a few more people echoing the broken ideas that have given us the highest divorce rate in human history, a dangerously self-centered materialistic society, and a world ready to self-destruct in nuclear war.

We can change our world, only if we continue to believe and live the very different values of Jesus' kingdom. If you seniors can model joyful loving families and lifelong marriage covenants right in the middle of today's sexual wilderness and marital agony, then you will change our world. If you seniors can model Jesus' costly concern for justice for the poor in the midst of uncaring affluence and selfish materialism, you will change our world. If you seniors dare to live Jesus' way of love for enemies in a costly challenge to nationalistic militarism and nuclear madness, you will change our world.

What a fantastic opportunity. What a tremendous challenge.

But you will never even get started on this task of transformation unless you keep perfectly clear the fact that kingdom values are radically different from the values of modern society. If you remember that, and if you resolve to put the kingdom ahead of everything else, ahead of money and status, ahead of security and convenience, ahead of power and nationalism, you will glorify the King of Kings. And in the process, you will have the time of your life.

Chapter 3: **Uncle Jesse**

[My admiration for my Uncle Jesse Sider led to an interview and his agreement that I should publish his story. After *Moody Monthly* first printed this piece in June, 1984, magazines around the world asked to reprint it. I never preached this piece as a sermon (although I often used parts of it in larger lectures). But one reader wrote to me sharing her belief that this little article was perhaps the most important item I had ever written.]

I ALWAYS CALLED HIM "Uncle Jesse." As a teenager, I thought of him as that friendly uncle with the shock of white hair and warm smile that everyone in my home congregation respected. We all knew that Uncle Jesse had to raise his two daughters by himself because his wife had been institutionalized for mental illness for as long as any of us could remember. But I never thought much about that—as a teenager, that is. His warmth and joy seldom betrayed deeper pain.

I have traveled a long way from the southern Ontario farmlands where Uncle Jesse still lives. But more and more often in more recent years, my thoughts have returned to Uncle Jesse. I have been married now for twenty-six years. As I have experienced the ecstasy, the pain, and the renewed joy of a growing, fulfilling marriage, I have wondered what it must have been like for Uncle Jesse to live alone for thirty years of married life. As I have watched marriages crumble because they were not "fulfilling," I have wondered what kept Uncle Jesse married for thirty years while his wife Lydia lived fifty miles away in a mental hospital.

Recently, I decided to ask him. So last Christmas, while visiting my family in Ontario, I interviewed him. (Here—largely in his own words—is the story of this devout southern Ontario farmer and the young woman he loved.)

Jesse and Lydia had been friends since childhood. They went to the same Brethren in Christ Church full of hard-working farmers. "I had strong attractions to her when I was pretty young yet, and she was young yet. We went together a little, broke off a little, and went together again. The second time she seemed to be a little hesitant. I had prayed about it, and I told the Lord that I would not go back to see her again unless she made some overture to me first. This happened, very unexpectedly to me. She did write me a letter, and invite me to come back, and she was quite serious this time." After a five year courtship, they finally got married on September 9, 1931.

Lydia had turned twenty-one three days earlier—the Wingers had a family idea that you shouldn't get married until you reached twenty-one. Jesse was twenty-two. "To me she was the one in the world," he told me. "And I think I kept that right to the end."

The first seven years of life together were good—"for both of us, as far as I know," Uncle Jesse said. In 1933, their first child, Anna Mae, arrived. Then on the morning of December 30, 1935, a second daughter, Ruth, was born. Back then, mothers normally gave birth at home. "That evening we had quite a lot of company," Jesse recalls, "which was wrong, I see now. Childbearing being kind of easy for her, she really had a good time that night."

But the next morning, something was obviously wrong. Physically, Lydia was in great health. But she behaved in a strange way. She would ask for something, and then, a moment later, ask for the exact opposite. The doctor recommended total rest.

Mental illness had invaded a happy marriage. For two and a half years, Lydia was able to live at home. She was clearly not normal. Her careless housekeeping and lack of concern for the baby were new and strange. For a time, however, she remained fairly stable.

Then in the middle of 1938, Lydia "really let loose and just became quite unmanageable at home. She had all kinds of ideas.

One morning she announced that I was not her husband. She said we weren't lawfully married—we weren't married at all."

They were living in a double house. So Lydia moved in with Uncle Andrew's family next door. "That kind of kept it, well, so it was livable."

One morning while Uncle Jesse was milking the cows, Lydia heard some hunters in the woods. When she heard a gun go off, she announced that that was Jesse. "He was all right, he was a good fellow, but he's gone, he shot himself," she declared.

With that, she came over to their own side of the house. Jesse came in to find Lydia lying on the floor, in front of the space heater. He washed and got ready for breakfast, and as soon as he left the room, she went back over to Uncle Andrew's.

In January of 1939, Jesse finally took her to the Hamilton hospital, one of the best psychiatric hospitals in Southern Ontario. The government would have covered the costs. But Uncle Jesse wanted to pay it himself. And he did—for thirty years.

At first, Uncle Jesse kept checking with the doctors each week when he visited Lydia, believing that his wife would soon be better. One day the doctor called him into the office.

"Your wife is not going to get any better," he announced grimly. "I think what you should do is go home, and make a new home. Take care of your girls, and forget about this woman. The girls don't even need to know she ever lived."

"Well, Doc!" Uncle Jesse protested. "I can go home and take care of the girls. But I can't forget her. She's part of me."

"Well, what are you going to tell the girls?" the doctor asked.

"I'm going to tell them that their mother's sick," Uncle Jesse retorted. The doctor let the matter drop.

For thirty years, Uncle Jesse drove the two hours to Hamilton every two or three weeks to visit the woman he had promised to love for better or worse till death them would part.

"Usually she was glad to see me," he recalled as we talked at Christmas, 1986. "Sometimes, though, she would hope I broke my neck on the way home. When that happened I'd go home and think, 'Well, what am I going to do? No use me going up there any more.' And then I couldn't help but think about her, and in a week or two I'd be back up again, and I could get an entirely different response."

One day he was out in the barn and he was praying for her, and he definitely felt that the Lord heard his prayer. The next day he found a letter from Lydia in the mailbox. She hadn't written home for years. But in her letter she took a very penitent attitude, saying she thought there had been a misunderstanding.

"I've often wished that I'd dropped everything and gone up right away to see her." But since he was busy on the farm that day, he didn't get to Hamilton until a few days later. He took the letter to show the doctor, thinking that this was the answer to his prayer.

"Don't bank too hard on it," the doctor warned. When Jesse saw her, Lydia's mood had changed drastically, "She reminded me of a teeter-totter. When she wrote the letter, she'd been on one side. But till I got up, she didn't know what she thought of me. Still, I actually think the whole ordeal strengthened me as far as the Lord was concerned."

After Lydia had been in the hospital a long time, the doctor again called Uncle Jesse in. He said, "Lydia says she wants a divorce."

"Well, if she had her right mind she wouldn't want a divorce," Uncle Jesse countered. "But I brought her up here to get help. So if you think a divorce is the answer—I'm sure in my mind it isn't, but if you think it is—I won't say no. If you think it's needed, then, go on with it."

The doctor never mentioned the subject again. Jesse thinks the doctors may have been testing to see if he would take a very rigid stance against a divorce. "Perhaps they were trying to determine whether or not I was contributing to Lydia's illness."

For many years, Uncle Jesse hoped and prayed that God would heal his wife. "Why she couldn't get healed, I don't know. That's one of the mysteries of this life." In 1953, the doctors suggested performing a lobotomy. (In this surgical operation, used for treating serious psychological disorders, a lobe of the brain is cut.)

For some inexplicable reason, the doctors chose to operate on Lydia the same day their older daughter Anna Mae was married. So Uncle Jesse couldn't be there when Lydia first came out of the anesthetic, as the doctors had requested.

But when he saw Lydia the next day, he marveled at the change in her. She asked questions about home, and other things she had never talked about in years. "This was the first thing that ever showed any signs of really helping her."

"Now don't expect her to stay like that," the doctors cautioned. "She'll drift back, but we hope she'll come back up to this point again in about six months."

After a little while, Uncle Jesse tried having her home for a week or two, but it didn't work well. One time Lydia wandered away from home and walked to my Mom's and Dad's farm about four miles away. "Some people were scared of her. It was a long pull there." My Dad went along as Uncle Jesse sadly returned her to the hospital.

Months later, he tried again. This time, things went much better. The doctors had been testing various kinds of medication for Lydia. Finally, they found the right combination. After twenty-nine years of separation, Lydia was home again. She was "not quite normal, but livable." Her sloppy appearance and religious indifference were painful reminders that Lydia was still not the woman he once knew. But she was far more reasonable and cooperative.

For three years Uncle Jesse gently cared for the woman he still thought of as his youthful sweetheart and bride.

"Then, one Thursday, Lydia got sick to her stomach. Four days later, she died of a ruptured appendix. Because of the operation in her brain, she never felt the pain that otherwise would have warned her that something was wrong."

The day before she died, Uncle Jesse visited her in the hospital. "Would you pray for me?" Lydia asked.

This was a bit unusual. "I'm sure she was a Christian before her mind got warped, but after that she could think most anything. While she was home those last years, she never showed any spiritual emotions at all, that I could see. And now she said, 'Would you pray for me?' And I said, 'Sure, I'll pray for you.'" The next day she was gone. Uncle Jesse said, "I felt as if this was the Lord's time to take her home. It all went so peacefully."

I cried as I listened to his story last Christmas. And I cried often as I listened later to the tape and wrote the story.

"Did you ever feel angry at the Lord?" I asked.

"I did right at first," he said. "I thought, 'This isn't fair; she was twenty-nine years old when this happened.' But that doesn't get you any place. All those years, never once did I feel that she was a burden. Oh sure, she was a burden, but I never felt that it was anything I should be relieved of. I loved her, and I did all I could."

"Do you think it would be harder today, to do what you did?" I asked him. "Thirty years back, divorce was seldom heard of, but today men abandon wives for far less reason."

"I can't understand the modern attitude," Uncle Jesse replied. "I chose a wife who I thought was it. Now why, after ten years, would I want to get rid of her for somebody else?"

"It looks like a very very difficult road to have been asked to walk," I suggested softly.

"Yes, especially if I had seen those thirty years ahead," he agreed. "I took her up there [to the Hamilton hospital] with the feeling that, like others I'd seen, she would be returning in three months or so. It just didn't work that way with her. We walk with the Lord one day at a time."

Uncle Jesse made a vow before God with the woman he loved to live in lifelong covenant for better or for worse. And it got much worse. But he kept that covenant, by God's grace, one day at a time.

Chapter 4: Staying Married in a Crazy World

[A sermon preached at the fiftieth wedding anniversary of my wife's parents, David and Fannie Lichti, at Hillcrest Mennonite Church. In New Hamburg, Ontario, on July 10, 1983.]

TODAY IS A DAY of special joy, celebration, and happiness for us in the Lichti family. We celebrate and praise God for the divine gift of fifty years of marriage. Fiftieth wedding anniversaries are increasingly unusual in our sad, confused society. That any couple today should reach that joyful landmark is a marvel of God's goodness. That three couples from Punkydoodles Corners should reach it together in the same year is reason for special joy. This is truly a day to revel and rejoice in the goodness of life that our Creator has given us. Even nature, on this glorious summer day, joins us in joyful exultation and praise. Truly this fiftieth wedding anniversary day is a day that the Lord has made. Let us be glad and rejoice in it.

Christian marriage is the best gift that God has given me after Jesus Christ, God's only Son. In fact, all through the Bible it is striking that God uses language borrowed from married life to talk about the intimate personal relationship that God has with you and me. Think of the Old Testament. God says God is married to Israel. Israel is God's virgin, God's bride, God's wife. Jesus performed his first recorded miracle at the marriage in Cana. Paul says that the church is the bride of Christ. And then Revelation 19, verse 9, gives us a picture of the final hope for which we yearn. And what is it? It is the marriage supper of the Lamb.

It is not an accident that the Bible frequently uses marriage language to talk about the personal relationship between God and God's people. Both relationships are intimate and personal, intended for deep joy, happiness, and ecstasy. According to the Bible the best clue about what it means to have a deep personal relationship with God comes from looking at the joy and the love between happily married couples. That is how special marriage is.

But every marriage experiences pain as well as joy. In the best of marriages there are storms of life, even occasionally, seasons of storms, when one tornado after another seems to tear through. If the storms are not too frequent, if God is good, if we work at it, we can clean up our fields and our forests. We can clean up our marriages. The storms can be the occasion for real growth, for deepening love, for the maturing of our relationship. But increasingly today devastating hurricanes seem to roar through our marriages tearing and ripping them apart. One of two marriages now ends in divorce. Even in the church, divorce is an ever more frequent reality.

Lifelong marriage is tough today, perhaps harder than before. The larger culture no longer supports marriage the way it used to. We no longer live in stable communities where it is the obvious, expected thing. Movies and television say marriage will not last. They tell us that affairs are the norm, that of course we divorce and remarry. Pop psychology tells us that we should think only of ourselves, that we ought to be meeting our own needs, that we have a right to self-fulfillment. If our spouse is not meeting our needs then, of course, we need to find somebody else who will. If we do not do that, we are not true to ourselves. We owe it to ourselves to be fulfilled. As Mennonites we are no longer isolated from the larger culture. The winds that blow through the total society affect all of us. Our society is crazy, it is messed up, it is falling apart at the point of the family. Lifelong marriage today is tough.

We need to stand and weep with those who have failed. God have mercy on us if those of us who still are married give in to the temptation to be proud, to be self-righteous, to be judgmental. If we are honest, we know very well that we all face the same temptations;

that we have all walked close to the precipice. But we need not despair. Christian faith has the resources to restore the family and the joy of lifelong marriage covenant.

We can keep lifelong marriage covenants today if we understand and grasp firmly the three C's of Christian marriage: Covenant, Cross, and Church.

First of all, the Covenant. What is the biblical understanding of Christian covenant? Genesis 2 and Matthew 19 help us understand. Genesis 2 is a fantastic story. Adam was not satisfied with the plants and animals and the things he could make. So God brings him Eve, bone of his bone, flesh of his flesh. Adam says, "Wow! That is what I have been looking for!" And it was very good! The Bible says that the man and the woman became one flesh. They became one, permanently. In Matthew 19 we see clearly that God was telling us in Genesis that marriage is a lifelong commitment. In Matthew 19 Jesus deals with the question of divorce. He quotes Genesis 2:24 and he says they become "one." The Greek there is really "one flesh." And then in verse 6 Jesus says, "What God has joined together, let no one separate." Let no person end this divinely established covenant of unity for life. Clearly Jesus is saying marriage is a lifelong commitment. It is not just for good times. It is for bad times, too.

It is for better, for worse, for richer, for poorer, for sickness and health, "until death do us part."

The best protection against giving up when there is pain (and there will be pain in our marriages at some time or another) is to be committed without reservation for the rest of one's life—"until death do us part." If that is clear, then we will struggle, we will cry, we will pray and God will bring us through—"until death do us part." What then, is a Christian marriage covenant? Well, first of all it is made before God—"what God has joined together." It is also made for life—"let no one separate," Jesus said. And it is to be made, you can be sure, with another person who is a believer. We need to make our marriage covenant with another Christian. Only Christians can make that kind of lifelong promise with the assurance that God will bring them through.

You know, the world has a cheap substitute for Christian marriage covenant. It is called contract. Sometimes the contract is explicit. Sometimes today people even talk about a contractual marriage. They agree on what each party will do. If the one party breaks the agreement and fails to keep their promises, then it is okay to dissolve the marriage because it was a contract, a limited contract. Often the contract is only implicit. We do not say explicitly that it is a contract but it is. We say, "Let's try it. Let's see if it works. Let's see if it feels good. Let's see if it meets my needs." In all that, of course, the hidden assumption of contract is that I have a right to self-fulfillment. If I am not getting my needs met, then the contract is off. If the other party does not meet my needs, then the contract is broken. Society's limited marriage contract is not Christian covenant. It is the devil's cheap substitute. It is a fraud. It is a trick—although Satan, of course, sells it to us with slick language and big promises. He says it brings freedom. He says it brings liberation. He says, "Society changes; you change; how on earth can you make a lifelong covenant?" I want to shout to my children, to all of our children, to all of us: "Let's not be deceived by Satan's lousy substitute." Let's choose unconditional solemn covenant before God rather than a limited liability contract. In God's name, let's choose Christian partners who will walk with us in Christian marriage covenant. That is the only foundation strong enough to bring us to the deep joy of fiftieth wedding anniversaries. Covenant, biblical covenant before God, is the first C of Christian marriage.

The second C is the Cross. We all know—anybody that has been married a few weeks knows—there is pain as well as joy in marriage. Each of us somehow is a proud, selfish, petty, silly sinner. We hurt each other and then, silly and stupid as we are, we try to cover it up or we try to blame the other person. We refuse to say we are sorry. It happens in the best of marriages. You know, finally, there is only one solution to all of that. It is a difficult solution. It is the solution at the heart of the gospel. It is the cross. It is costly forgiveness.

Ephesians 5 says that we are supposed to love our spouses—I think it applies to wives as well as husbands—we are supposed to love our spouses as Christ loved the church. How did Christ love the church? He died for it. He went to the cross. Why? Because you and I are such stinking sinners. That is why.

Every marriage has that kind of pain.

When we hurt each other and betray each other there are three options.

First of all, we can live with our anger. We can live with our resentment. We can let it build up and grow and even feed on it. That is one choice.

The second choice is what I call cheap forgiveness. We can pretend it really does not matter much. "Aw, shucks. It was nothing. I do not care. It is okay. It did not really hurt much." That is not really true. But you can try to play that game of pretense if you like.

There is a third choice and that is the only one that really works. It is costly forgiveness. That is the way of the cross. Pain, betrayal, selfishness and sin in marriage do matter. They hurt like hell. They tear us apart. Costly forgiveness responds to the hurt in marriage the same way that God responds to sin. God says it is serious. Indeed so serious that the death penalty has to be paid. And then God takes the death penalty upon Godself at the cross. God goes to the cross because God loves us in spite of our sinful failures. That kind of costly forgiveness is the only way to stay happily married for fifty years. When the hurt comes, we need to face it. We need to say it is bad because it is not nothing. It hurts. Then we can say, "I accept the pain that your betrayal, that your sin, brings upon me and I forgive you." That is the only way to reconciliation. You cannot pretend that you have not been hurt. You cannot wish it away. You can only embrace the pain and forgive. That allows the other person to say, "I am sorry." That allows healing and reconciliation to occur. How often do we need to do that? Husbands are to love their wives and wives are to love their husbands as Christ loves the church. How often does Christ forgive you? Seventy times seven and seventy times seven. How many times has Christ forgiven you in the past ten years? In the last fifty years? Well, that is the way that we need to go on forgiving our husbands and our wives.

The second C, the Cross, costly forgiveness, is closely related to the first C of covenant. The cross means never giving up. As long as we live, Christ stands there offering us forgiveness, repentance. God never says, "I have had enough of you. I have had enough of your stupidity, of your silliness, of your unfaithfulness, of your sin and your failures." God always stands there as long as we live, saying, "I will give you another chance." Taking the way of the cross in our marriages, loving our spouses as Christ loved the church, means never giving up, even in a difficult, painful time. This is not, I hasten to add, a recipe for sheer agony, for masochism. It is the only way to healing and to joy. It is the only way to happiness in marriage. Since pain and failure will always come, even in the best of marriages, the only way to restoration and joy is costly forgiveness. The second C, the cross, is the only path to renewed joy and healing.

Then finally, the third C, the Church. Young people may say: "All this sounds kind of scary. The demands seem very high. Lifelong commitment is a hard calling." They are right; it is. But remember, we are not alone. The risen Christ is in us. We have the power of God to keep our promises and we also have the love and support of the church, our last C. All of the other brothers and sisters in the body of Christ promise to help us and that is why we have church weddings rather than just going off by ourselves to elope. The wedding covenant is not just a solemn covenant between God and two persons. It is also a solemn covenant in front of the brothers and sisters. They all promise, by attending the wedding, to help us in that marriage covenant.

In Ephesians, chapter 5, verses 29 through 32, Paul quotes Genesis 2: "No one ever hated their own body, but they feed and care for their body, just as Christ does the church for we are members of his body. For this reason, a man will leave his father and mother and be united to his wife, and the two will become one flesh. This is a profound mystery—but I am talking about Christ and the church." Paul is saying that becoming one flesh in marriage is symbolic in some way of Christ's union with the church.

Notice, he says it symbolizes the union between Christ and the church, not the union between Christ and the individual Christian. We are not alone as individual Christians. We are part of the body. We are all united in the church with Christ, our bridegroom. That makes us one. As Paul says in 1 Corinthians 12:26, if one suffers, we all suffer; if one rejoices, we all rejoice. That is why we come together in the body of Christ to celebrate a wedding or to celebrate a fiftieth wedding anniversary.

But the other side is that we stand together too when there are tough times. That is what we promise every young couple who comes to be married in the church. We are responsible for each other's marriages. Everybody in a congregation is responsible if somebody's marriage fails. Did we pray or gossip? Did we cry or silently sneer? Did we gently counsel holding on or did we stay coldly silent?

There are lots and lots of ways that this third C, the church, is crucial today. We need much more emphasis in teaching for our young people on the beauty and joy of lifelong commitment in Christian marriage. We need more premarital counseling. I wish we would say in our churches that we will not marry anyone unless they have gone through several months of Christian marriage counseling. We need better post-marital counseling. We need to tell each other it is okay to get counseling if we are having struggles in our marriage.

You know, it is very easy to be too proud to do that. I think God has given Arbutus and me one of the best marriages I have seen. But there came a time a few years ago when we very badly needed counseling. But I was too proud to do that for quite a while. I knew that many marriages around us were in trouble and that they needed help. In fact, I was encouraging some of them to go and get counseling. But me? Thank God, after a while when I hurt enough, I was ready to do that. Six months of marriage counseling for Arbutus and myself with a wonderful Christian counselor was a tremendously important healing experience.

Marriage Encounter is another way that the church can help marriages. In Marriage Encounter, couples come together for a weekend to learn new techniques for tasting each other's feelings and for understanding each other. Arbutus and I did a Marriage Encounter and after that we tried new kinds of ways to understand and feel each other's feelings. We used to pray in each other's shoes.

There are lots of ways that the church can help strengthen marriage today. And, of course, when a marriage does fail, we need to cry together, weep together, and forgive each other.

Satan, you know, is a clever liar. He says marriages used to last because people had no other option. They hated each other. They lived parallel lives and they just stayed together because of custom. Now that is partly true and partly a lie. But this third C, the church, gives us a way of handling the truth in this charge. I am not saying we should live forever with a terrible marriage, merely enduring the agony. I am saying there are ways to work at the pain, the failures, the hurts in each of our marriages. The church can and must help us do that. You can share your pain with the pastor or with a Christian marriage counselor. You can go to a Marriage Encounter weekend. Forgiveness, healing, and renewal are possible in your marriage. The body of Christ, the church, is the support that God gives for lifelong marriage covenant.

Apart from salvation itself, Christian marriage is the most wonderful gift that God has given me in life. Christian marriage is a tremendous gift from the Creator to us. But it is not always a bed of roses. It involves pain as well as joy. Covenant, cross, and church are absolutely essential for Christian marriage today.

If as a church we will resolve anew to strengthen Christian marriage in the body of Christ, then we can promise our children and grandchildren that they too can reach the joyous landmark of a fiftieth wedding anniversary filled with the mature love that comes when one man and one woman walk together through the joy and pain of life, loving and crying together, forgiving and rejoicing, forgetting and exulting together. And we can all look forward, thank God, to that great marriage celebration when we will gather together to sing and rejoice at the final marriage supper of the Lamb.

Chapter 5: Preaching Holiness
in a Promiscuous Age

[A sermon preached sometime in the early 1980s, but I cannot locate the exact place or date.]

I MUST START WITH a confession. My title is not quite accurate. "Preaching Holiness in a Relativistic Age" would be more precise. But that's not a very jazzy title. These days, everything, even sermon titles, must have a little sex appeal. But if you came expecting a lot of titillating stories about promiscuity, you will be disappointed.

Two recent personal experiences illustrate the problem I want to discuss this morning.

In March, 1990, I had the privilege of participating in Korea in a convocation of the World Council of Churches dealing with Justice, Peace and the Integrity of Creation. To my surprise, I was asked to chair one of the drafting committees. As we worked together, I pointed out that all the discussion of sin in the draft document focused on the horizontal dimension—on the way that sin is a dreadful violation of the neighbor. With all of that, of course, I agree. But I pointed out that sin is also rebellion against a Holy, Righteous God, a violation of the just commandments of the Divine Judge who hates sin. Some dismissed such language as paternalistic oppression, insisting that we focus only on God as loving, forgiving, accepting, nurturing. Others, I'm sure, ignored my plea for other reasons. But language about sin as a violation of God's holiness—it never made it into the final document.

A few weeks later, I was sharing my concerns about the contemporary church with a small circle of younger evangelicals. I talked about my fear that the radical subjectivism and relativism of the larger society were creeping into the church, even into evangeli-cal circles. I said the dominant value of current American culture is that what feels good to me is right for me. And God have mercy on anyone who dares to be so legalistic and medieval as to suggest that the righteous commandments of the Holy Creator of the galaxies are divine commands to me no matter how I feel.

I won't try to describe what all happened at that point. You can use your imagination. I'm still limping. We had quite a de-bate. One person almost walked out. Another person said that he wanted to focus all his attention on God's love. All he could man-age, he said, were two convictions: that he should love God with all his heart and his neighbor as himself.

Of course, I agreed that this double conviction (it wasn't clear that we would dare use the word *commandment*) is of course the heart of the whole matter. Our whole Christian life should flow out of gratitude for the astonishing, unmerited love of God in Christ. Because of that love, we can love God in return and our neighbor as well. But don't Jesus and Paul go on to tell us that loving neighbor means obeying God's commands not to violate the neighbor through adultery, robbery, gossip, or neglect of justice? In this small evangelical circle, just as at the World Council of Churches convocation, I sensed a powerful hesitation to face the blazing holiness and righteous demands of Almighty God who is holy and demanding just as well as forgiving and merciful. I'm afraid the modern world is making it hard for us to hear one whole aspect of biblical truth.

How has this happened? I can't do an intellectual history of the last few centuries in the next few minutes, so I can't answer that question adequately here. But I do want to point to a few of the key developments.

The Enlightenment's demand for absolute human autonomy is at the heart of the problem. Rejecting revelation as the source of ethics, Kant and the Enlightenment grounded ethics in au-tonomous humanity. Persons rather than God became the center of the universe. Then a variety of philosophical determinisms reduced ethical ideas to a mere relativistic by-product of this or that. Marx insisted that all ethical ideas were merely the by-product of economic life and thus totally relative. Freud preferred to reduce our values to psychological conditioning. Lofty values are merely the result of our economy or toilet training. As Bertrand Russell, one of the great secular philosophers of the twentieth century said so eloquently: "Those who have the best poison gas will have the ethics of the future." All is relative.

And if you want to know how it all works, just ask the sociologists of knowledge. They will tell you how it happens. If you grow up in a society where the influential others are witch doctors, you will believe in witchcraft. And if you grow up among allegedly scientific secular humanists, you will think like secular humanists. All is relative.

Current American culture, of course, adds its own delightful spin to this prevailing relativism. Pop psychology assures us that whatever feels good is right for me. I have a right to self-fulfillment and if my spouse is not meeting my "needs," then I had better find someone else who will or I may do terrible things to my psyche.

Christians quickly step forward to provide theological rationales for this prevailing relativism. One preacher largely ignores sin and develops a gospel of self-esteem. Another ignores justice for the poor and preaches a gospel of wealth. Some radical feminists dismiss language about God's justice and holiness as oppressive paternalism. And Tammy Bakker shares her spiritual wisdom in a book with the wonderful title *I Gotta Be Me*.

Mixed in with all this tragic nonsense is a set of confusions that further complicate the issues. Pluralism is confused with relativism, tolerance with subjectivism, the universality of sin with acceptance of sin.

I understand the reality of religious pluralism and vigorously defend everybody's right to believe what they choose. And I want to be tolerant of different views in the sense that I respect those who believe very differently than I do. But that does not mean that one idea is as good as another. I can respect your right to think whatever you choose and still believe passionately that your ideas are dead wrong. Society should tolerate all ideas, but that does not mean that all ideas are equally true. But again and again, people confuse tolerance and relativism. A. W. Tozer has a powerful line that sums it up: "Truth is slain to provide a feast to celebrate the marriage of heaven and hell." (Warren Wiersbe, ed., *The Best of A. W. Tozer* [Grand Rapids: Baker, 1978], 72.)

People also regularly confuse the universality of sin and the acceptance of sin. How many times have you heard somebody object to a clear biblical condemnation of some specific sin, whether economic injustice or sexual misconduct, with the plea: "But we are all sinners." If I hear that confused response one more time, I fear I may go theologically berserk. The fact that we all sin and fail to keep God's law does not mean that we should not object to sin. It simply means that as we condemn racism or adultery, we also cast ourselves on God's grace to ask forgiveness for our own failures.

Probably the greatest temptation of the church over the ages has been slowly and often unconsciously to conform to surrounding culture rather than submit to the fullness of God's revealed word. Always of course one aspect of biblical truth is affirmed while another is obscured and neglected.

God is certainly love—overwhelming, astounding love. That is at the core of the biblical revelation of the nature of God. But the Bible also tells us that God is holy and just. The Bible says God hates sin. Tragically a variety of modern confusions make it difficult for contemporary Christians to hear this other side of biblical truth.

Let me remind you of the way every stream of biblical revelation affirms the holiness of God. As I quote a series of texts, let the awesome holiness of our Almighty Creator sink deeper into your being.

Here is how the prophet Isaiah describes his encounter with the Holy One in Isaiah 6:1–5.

> In the year that King Uzziah died I saw the Lord, high and exalted, seated on a throne; and the train of his robe filled the temple. Above him were seraphim, each with six wings: With two they covered their faces, with two they covered their feet, and with two they were flying. And they were calling to one another: "Holy, holy, holy

is the Lord Almighty; the whole earth is full of his glory."
At the sound of their voices the doorposts and thresh-
olds shook and the temple was filled with smoke. "Woe
to me!" I cried. "I am ruined! For I am a man of unclean
lips, and I live among a people of unclean lips, and my
eyes have seen the King, the Lord Almighty."

After David raped Beersheba and then murdered her husband,
he repented and called on God for forgiveness. He could very rightly have stressed how terrible had been his violation of his neighbor.
But Psalm 51 emphasizes his rebellion against a holy God.

For I know my transgressions, and my sin is always before me. Against you, you only have I sinned, and done
what is evil in your sight; so you are right in your verdict
and justified when you judge. (Psalm 51: 3–4)

I have recently rediscovered the power and beauty of Psalm
119's praise and love for God's holy commandments. Listen to
verses 9 through 16:

How can a young person stay on the path of purity?
By living according to your word. I seek you with all
my heart; do not let me stray from your commands. I
have hidden your word in my heart, that I might not
sin against you. Praise be to you, Lord; teach me your
decrees. With my lips I recount all the decrees that come
from your mouth. I rejoice in following your statutes as
one rejoices in great riches. I meditate on your precepts
and consider your ways. I delight in your decrees; I will
not neglect your word.

Nor does the emphasis on God's holiness and demand for
obedience end with the Old Testament. Those who do not obey
Jesus' command to feed the hungry will hear the awful words:

Depart from me, you who are cursed, into the eternal
fire prepared for the devil and his angels (Matthew 25:4).

And when Jesus leaves his disciples and gives them the Great
Commission, he tells them that making disciples of all nations

means not just baptizing people but also "teaching them to observe all that I have commanded you."

St. Paul, that great apostle of grace and freedom, never hesitated to underline God's holy hatred of sin. Romans 1:18 says,

> The wrath of God is being revealed from heaven against all the ungodliness and wickedness of people who suppress the truth by their wickedness.

And consider Galatians 5:19–21:

> The acts of the flesh are obvious: sexual immorality, impurity and debauchery; idolatry and witchcraft; hatred, discord, jealousy, fits of rage, selfish ambition, dissentions, factions and envy, drunkenness, orgies and the like. I warn you, as I did before, that those who live like this will not inherit the kingdom of God.

God's word is clear. God is both loving and just, both merciful and holy, both nurturing and demanding, both gentle with sinners and furious with sin.

A promiscuous relativistic age wants to hear only one half of that. My question for all of us this morning is this: Will you, will I, also dare to preach and live God's holiness? It is a scary call because the people do not want to hear this tough love. But if we fail to preach the full biblical word, we will both ruin the church and deny our Lord.

Ezekiel 33 is a powerful passage about the awesome responsibility of the preacher, God's spokesperson. The preacher is like the watchman placed by God before the people to warn them of coming danger. If she sees danger descending and blows the warning trumpet, then those who ignore the warning are responsible for their own destruction. But if the watchman fails to blow the warning trumpet, then he is responsible for everyone's destruction.

Listen to Ezekiel 33:7–9—listen to it as a word to pastors in a relativistic age:

> Son of man, I have made you a watchman for the people of Israel; so hear the word I speak and give them warning from me. When I say to the wicked, "You wicked

person, you will surely die," and you do not speak out to dissuade them from their ways, that wicked person will die for their sin, but I will hold you accountable for their blood. But if you warn the wicked person to turn from their ways, and they do not do so, they will die for their sin, though you yourself will be saved.

Do you have the guts to preach all that God's word says about holiness, purity, and obedience to God's righteous commands? Of course you don't. Neither do I. But we can decide as ministers of the word to do exactly that and then turn to God for the courage.

A. W. Tozer has a lovely ordination prayer that expresses all this with pointed lucidity:

Save me from the curse that lies dark across the face of the modern clergy, the curse of compromise, of imitation, of professionalism. Save me from the error of judging a church by its size, its popularity or the amount of its yearly offering. Help me to remember that I am a prophet—not a promoter, not a religious manager, but a prophet. Let me never become a slave to crowds. . . . I am thy servant to do Thy will, and that will is sweeter to me than position or riches or fame and I choose it above all things on earth or in heaven. (Warren Wiersbe, ed., *The Best of A. W. Tozer* [Grand Rapids: Baker, 1978], 78–79.)

Only if you reach that point of unconditional personal consecration can you be a preacher of holiness. You cannot preach holiness and live in timidity or impurity.

So my final plea is that you and I fall down together before our Holy God and beg for both forgiveness and personal holiness. Create in me a clean heart, O God. That means surrendering every corner of my life, every secret ambition, every hidden seductive temptation to the searing, cleansing Divine Purity. O Lord, I do, forgive my hesitation.

For a little while, of course, it is possible to talk a good talk even if we don't walk the walk. But not for long. Only people who yearn to be holy can preach about holiness.

So I beg you. Let God's holiness burn through your own soul until you stand surrendered, totally, unconditionally surrendered, before God Almighty.

And then out of that personal transformation, resolve to be a faithful preacher of holiness in a relativistic, promiscuous age.

Don't draw back from that terrifying task. Your decision will affect the future of the church. And the Holy Creator of the galaxies will be your strength and shield.

Chapter 6: Thinking Clearly About the Finite and the Infinite

[A sermon preached at my home congregation, Diamond Street Mennonite Church in Philadelphia, on April 2, 1988 and then at New Mercies Mennonite Church also in Philadelphia on June 30, 1996.]

WHEN YOU HEARD THE title of this sermon, some of you probably thought: "Come off it , Ron. Get off your high horse and cut the high falutin' nonsense."

Okay, if you prefer, I can title this sermon: "What is sin all about?"

But I believe thinking about sin in terms of the finite and infinite really helps. Think about the meaning of the word *finite*. It comes from the Latin word *finis,* which means end. Finite things have an end. This pulpit ends. Every honeymoon ends. The earth is very big but it has an end. The solar system is much bigger but it also has an end. Everything in the created order has an end.

Only one thing has no end: God. God is infinite. The word *infinite* means without end. There is no end to God's knowledge because God is all-knowing. There is no end to God's power because God is all-powerful. There is no end to God's presence because God is everywhere. God is infinite.

As we look at Genesis and Romans, we see that the heart of sin is making some finite, created things god instead of accepting God himself, the infinite one, as God. We human beings love to make ourselves the center of everything. We love to play God. We like to make our husband or our wife or our children do whatever we want. We like to sit in a meeting and think that our comments were the most important, just the ones that got the meeting going. We like to think that we are more beautiful or handsome than our friends.

This is really pretty silly!

One morning this week, I was sitting on my prayer cushion having devotions. I was excited about all the things happening in my life. And there were many good things God was allowing me to do.

Then I began to think about how tiny and insignificant I really am. I am just one small person in Germantown, which is just one neighborhood in a city with dozens of neighborhoods. And Philadelphia is just one city in a country of 240 million people. And the United States is just one country on our planet with seven billion people. And the earth is just one of several planets revolving around our sun. And our sun is just one of billions of stars in our galaxy. And our galaxy is just one of perhaps 200 billion galaxies and each galaxy has billions of stars. So there I sat on my little cushion in a tiny part of Philadelphia in one country on a tiny planet in one small solar system in one small galaxy: feeling important!

I'm not exactly infinite. I am very, very limited, very, very small!

Only God is infinite. God knows everything about all the people and all the things in the billions of planets and stars in 200 billion galaxies. It takes millions of light years for light to travel to our planet from distant stars. But God is here and there and everywhere in the whole universe all at the same time!

It is really very silly. But we seem to want to take God's place. The Bible says we want to be the center of everything.

Genesis 3:1–19 tell us that the first thing Satan did was to make the woman doubt God. Is God really God? In verse 4, satan assures Eve that even though God said they would die if they disobeyed, they will not die. So the woman began to doubt God. Notice verse five. Satan promises that if she disobeys God, she will be like God! That was a big lie. You wonder how they could believe such nonsense. But we can accept almost anything if it makes us look good.

Verse 6 says that they looked at the tree of knowledge and it looked great. There was no obvious reason not to eat the fruit except that God had said they should not. So they placed their tiny limited reason above the command of the infinite God. Instead of letting God set the rules, they made their own rules even though they were small and finite and God is infinite.

The result of course is that Adam and Eve messed up everything. They messed up their relationship with God. When God came down, they ran and hid. When a finite person tries to take God's place, fellowship with God is broken.

They also messed up all relations with themselves and the earth. Adam blames Eve and Eve blames the snake. What a family fight they must have had that night! Even the earth is messed up: the ground is cursed and thorns spring up.

You see, the created world is finite, but still very good. The Bible gives us a fantastic picture of joy and goodness in the garden of Eden. God wants us to enjoy this good earth: fruit trees, flowers, and the ecstasy of a man and woman living together in love and joy. But we can enjoy the good finite earth only if we don't make it more important than it is. If we make these good finite things more important than God, then we spoil even the goodness of the finite.

Romans 1, verse 18 and following has a profound theological discussion about the nature of sin. Romans 1 makes the same basic point as Genesis 3. Verse 23 says that persons replace the glory of the infinite God with finite things. We make images of people and birds to worship instead of God. Verse 25 shows that we worship the creatures rather than the Creator. Verse 28 says we will not accept God as God.

In truth, only the all-powerful, all-knowing God is infinite. We are tiny, limited, finite. And the heart of sin is to want to play God, to try to place ourselves at the center of the universe. So we place our weak reasoning above God's knowledge and revelation. We place our desires above God's commands.

Now all that still sounds very abstract. It's just theory. Maybe it sounds like just a dry theology lecture!

So let's make it concrete. Think of a junior high schoolgirl who says to herself, "I am more pretty than my classmate." And then they see somebody in the next class who is prettier than both of them. And they are both jealous. You know what? Both girls would really like to be just a little more pretty than even the most stunning movie star. In fact what each girl wants is to be the prettiest of them all. You know the children's story: "Mirror, mirror on the wall, who's the prettiest of them all?"

I do not mean to pick on the young women. When we have a church ballgame, I would like to have the best home run and catch the most difficult line drive. If it could be arranged, it would be nice to be a little better than Michael Jordan or Wilt Chamberlain at basketball. The same applies with grades. I'd be glad to be a little smarter than Albert Einstein. We are never satisfied with what we are. We always want a little more. And what we really want to be is to be God. We don't want to accept our finitude. We proudly reject our limitations.

Let's think about four specific areas and see how we refuse to accept our being finite, limited. And as a result we mess things up. Let's think about four ways that we worship the creature instead of God.

First, marriage. Every husband and wife is finite, limited. Except for one husband in the world, somebody else has a prettier wife. Except for one husband in the world, somebody else has a smarter wife. Except for one husband in the world, somebody else has a kinder wife. If we don't accept the fact that our husband or wife is finite, limited, indeed quite imperfect, we are in for big trouble.

My wife Arbutus is a wonderful person. But she's not perfect. In fact on Tuesday and Saturday mornings, she's a long way from being perfect.

So I can do one of two things. I can accept her with her limitations and remember that I too am far, far from perfect and have no right to suppose that I deserve the most beautiful, the most intelligent, the most loving, the most thoughtful wife in the world.

Or I can secretly long for a perfect and infinitely wonderful, infinitely fabulous wife. If I do the latter, our marriage is in big trouble. If I do that, I will keep wanting other women who are more intelligent or more kind or more sexy or whatever.

I need to accept my finitude and her finitude. Then I can rejoice in the wonderful person Arbutus actually is and accept the fact that she is not perfect. That's okay! You know, it looks like Arbutus is never really going to fall in love with cleaning the house. It's okay if Arbutus is less of an interior decorator than someone else. It's okay that I am less handsome by far than Asa. It's okay if my spouse or I am a little fatter or a little skinnier or . . . Being finite is okay. Only God can satisfy my desire for the infinite. If I look for the infinite in my wife or in any finite thing, then I mess up everything.

Or take a second area, material things.

Material things are very good. God wants us to live in a land flowing with milk and honey. Material things are so good that the biblical picture of heaven is that of a banquet, a grand feast! But it is so easy to make finite, limited material things more important than God, to let them become my god. We let them take the place of the infinite God.

So we make money more important than Sunday worship or small group. We want more and more clothes, bigger houses, and better cars. And we forget God to get these things. Sometimes we destroy our families to get these things. We want more and more and more. We will kill to get more. Drug lords will destroy hundreds and thousands of people so they can have big houses and cars and billion-dollar bank accounts. They worship money. None of us are that bad, of course, but the same temptation faces all of us in smaller ways.

The tragedy is that the more we try to find our ultimate happiness in material things, the more unhappy we become. So wealthy kids in rich families go on drugs looking for happiness.

The reason we cannot find ultimate satisfaction in material things is that God made us so we can only find full happiness and satisfaction in God, the Infinite One. Material things are good as long as we keep them in their place. But they are less important by far than persons and God. Once we start to worship material things, everything is messed up.

Number three, nationalism. There is a good kind of healthy patriotism. This is a lovely land. I enjoy singing the words, "This land is your land, this land is my land." But it is so tempting to make our nation the ultimate good instead of just a finite good. So we worship our country. We become blind to its faults. We think it is the last best hope for earth. That's silly! The last best hope for earth is the infinite God.

Finally, aging. Why are we so afraid of admitting our age? Of getting gray hair? Perhaps it is because we don't want to accept our being finite and limited.

Since the fall, God has declared that all persons will live for a few short years and then die. Our bodies will decay. That does not mean that we have no hope. We will have resurrected bodies and live forever in Christ's coming kingdom when he returns.

But for now, our teeth decay, , our eyesight dims, our hair falls out, our energy slowly slips away.

We can respond to that in two ways. We can respond in a proud, sinful way. We can try to deny our being finite. We can buy wigs, we can get face-lifts to take out the wrinkles, we can dye our hair to hide the gray. What we are really trying to do is pretend we are not finite, limited. We are trying to hide the fact that we will die. We are really trying to be God. We would like to be infinite. We would like to be like the infinite, immortal God who does not decay and who never dies.

There is another way to respond to aging. We can accept the fact that we are finite, limited. We can accept the fact that only God is infinite and immortal. It's okay that our bodies wear out. It's okay that the young men can run faster than I can. (That was very clear at the last church retreat!)

My mother and father have lived good lives. But they are eighty-two and their bodies are weakening and that feels sad. But it's okay. I don't think I'll pray for their healing when they get really sick. Rather I will pray that they are at peace and feel a powerful presence of the Lord as their bodies get weaker and weaker. It is simply a fact. Human life here on earth is finite, limited. That's okay.

To proudly ask that this body of clay last forever is to reject the result of the sin of Adam and Eve. It is to try to be God.

One final point in conclusion.

There is a reason why we keep seeking for "better" spouses, bigger cars, longer life—more, more, more.

God made us with a longing for the Infinite. St. Augustine said our hearts are restless until they rest in God. We have a God-shaped place at the center of our hearts. Nothing finally can satisfy that longing except the living, infinite God.

No wife or husband, no matter how wonderful, can satisfy that longing for the infinite God. No car or house, no matter how new and improved, can satisfy that longing for the infinite God. No knowledge or scientific discovery or technology, no matter how fantastic, can satisfy that longing for the infinite God. No political power, no matter if it controls the whole earth or the whole galaxy, can satisfy that longing for the infinite God.

The human tragedy, the core of sin, is that we try to satisfy this longing for the infinite God with little tiny finite things. So we go for more and more sex, more and more money, trying to satisfy our need for the infinite creator through finite creatures. And it never works!

Let's stop looking for our ultimate happiness in the wrong places. Let's turn our hearts to the Infinite, Almighty God.

PART TWO: Holistic Ministry, Justice, and Peace

Chapter 7: **Words and Deeds in Apartheid South Africa**

[My plenary address to the South African Christian Leadership Assembly (SACLA) in Pretoria, South Africa, on July 14, 1979. SACLA brought together about five thousand South African Christians from almost all the races and denominations to struggle with the issue of apartheid. Sadly, it took another decade and a half before Nelson Mandela was released from prison and apartheid ended. This address was published in *The Journal of Theology for Southern Africa* (December, 1979, 31–50).]

MY TITLE, "WORDS AND Deeds," is general enough that I could justify talking about almost anything without too much distortion. Under "words," one could certainly wax eloquent about theology, preaching, and evangelism. Under "deeds," one could urge concern for relief, development, and social justice. But I only have forty minutes so there is not time to discuss everything, even though, when I have finished, you may think I tried to do just that.

So I want to limit myself to two issues: evangelism and the search for social justice. It would be quite wrong to think that evangelism involves merely words and the search for justice only deeds. Both evangelism and the search for justice involve both words and deeds. But verbal proclamation is certainly critical to the task of evangelism. And action is crucial to the search for justice. Both by the words of evangelism and the deeds of seeking justice we witness to the God revealed in Scripture.

It's no secret however that there is a lot of sharp disagreement and bitter controversy in the church today over the nature of evangelism and its relationship to the search for justice.

I think I should honestly tell you my basic viewpoint right at the beginning. I believe very strongly the church today should vastly increase its evangelistic activity. I believe that every person in this world needs to hear the Good News that God loves them, that Jesus died for their sins, and that they can enter into a personal, living relationship with the risen Lord Jesus and join his new community of disciples. No matter how poor and oppressed one is, no matter how affluent and oppressive one may be, the risen Lord Jesus invites you to repent of your sins, join Jesus' new society of disciples and let the blessed Holy Spirit transform your life. But I also must confess with equal vigor that I believe the church today should vastly increase its commitment to the search for justice in society. The same Bible that tells us God loves us sinners so much that God's Son suffered on the cross for our sake also insists that God is on the side of the poor and demands justice for the oppressed. The God of Scripture abhors socioeconomic systems and political structures that are unfair and insists that those who try to worship God without doing justice are an abomination. Grateful obedience and faithful witness to the Almighty Sovereign revealed in Scripture must involve both evangelism and justice.

But what is evangelism? The literal meaning of the New Testament word to evangelize is simply to announce Good News. So we must pose another question: What is the Good News? Jesus' answer to that question is quite clear. According to the Gospels, the core of Jesus' proclamation of the Good News was simply that the kingdom of God was at hand. The introduction to Jesus' life in Mark 1:14–15 reads: "Jesus went into Galilee proclaiming the good news of God. 'The time has come . . . The kingdom of God has come near. Repent, and believe the good news.'" Over and over and over again the Gospels define the content of the Good News as the kingdom that became present in the person and work of Jesus (Mark 1:14-15; Matthew 4:23; 24:14; Luke 4:43; 16:16). According to Jesus, then, the Gospel is the Good News of the kingdom.

But what was the nature of the kingdom Jesus proclaimed? Was it an invisible kingdom in the hearts of individuals? Was it a new political regime of the same order as Rome? One hesitates to simplify difficult questions about which scholars have written dozens of learned tomes. But let me try. The kingdom comes wherever Jesus overcomes the power of evil. That happens most visibly in the church. But it also happens in society at large because Jesus is Lord of the world as well as the church (Matthew 28:18; Ephesians 1:20–22; Revelation 1:5). The "kingdom of God" is a dynamic concept that refers to the kingly reign or rule of God that broke into history decisively in the incarnation and will come in its fullness at our Lord's return.

To understand what Jesus meant by the kingdom of God, we need to remember the ancient Jewish hope for the coming Messianic Age. Jews divided world history Into the Old Age of evil and injustice and the new Messianic Age of justice and peace. The Jews of Jesus' day longed for the days of the coming Messiah who would end the old age and begin the new by throwing off the yoke of the oppressive Romans. At the beginning of the New Age, the dead would be resurrected and God's Spirit would be poured out on all flesh.

When Jesus of Nazareth announced the welcome news that he was the long-expected Messiah, large crowds flocked to him. But the religious leaders and Roman oppressors quickly crucified him for blasphemy and treason. Jesus had failed.

Then God raised him from the dead. Jesus' resurrection confirmed his claim to be the Messiah. Jesus' resurrection and the gift of the Holy Spirit at Pentecost demonstrated that Jesus had been right in saying that the New Messianic Age had begun to invade the Old Age. The resurrection and Pentecost confirmed Jesus' announcement that the kingdom of God had become visible in Jesus and his new community.

Jesus, you see, was not an isolated, individualistic prophet. He established a radically new kind of community or society. He gathered a circle of disciples around him and they began to live a set of values sharply different from those of the rest of society.

Jesus' new community and Jesus' new values fundamentally challenged the status quo at almost every point. Jesus horrified the legalistic Pharisees preoccupied with meticulous observance of the Mosaic law by teaching that God freely forgives even the worst of sinners. Jesus surprised rulers of all kinds delighted with their powerful domination of their subjects by his revolutionary call for servant leadership. Jesus upset men, happy with easy divorce laws that allowed them to get rid of their wives for many reasons, with his insistent reminder that God intended one man and one woman to live together in lifelong, joyful union. Jesus angered the zealots fired with revolutionary zeal to kill Roman oppressors with the call to love even enemies. Jesus defied social codes that treated women as inferiors who did not dare touch a copy of the Torah by treating women as equals and teaching them theology. And Jesus terrified the economic establishment with his summons to apply the ancient biblical teaching on the Jubilee.

A closer look at Jesus' announcement of the Jubilee will show more clearly how Jesus' new kingdom fundamentally challenged the status quo.

When the Israelites first entered Canaan, the land had been divided fairly equally among the tribes and families. God gave the law of Jubilee, described in Leviticus 25, to make sure that great extremes of wealth and poverty did not arise among his people. Every fifty years all land was to return to the original owners— without compensation. Since land was the basic form of capital in ancient Israel, the law of Jubilee was designed to guarantee that each family had the capital to earn their own way.

But what basis is there for thinking that the Jubilee was central to Jesus' thought and ministry? The basic evidence is in Luke 4:16–30—St. Luke's programmatic account of the dramatic encounter in the synagogue at Nazareth at the beginning of Jesus' public ministry. Jesus read from Isaiah 61:1 and claimed that he was the fulfillment of these words:

> The Spirit of the Lord is upon me because he has anoint-
> ed me to proclaim good news to the poor. He has sent
> me to proclaim freedom for the prisoner, and recover of
> sight for the blind, to set the oppressed free, to proclaim
> the year of the Lord's favor.

That's one crucial part of the way Jesus himself defined his mission.

But what did he mean? There is good evidence to think that Jesus meant to announce the Jubilee.

A very recent dissertation completed at the University of Basel by an evangelical scholar, Robert Sloan, has shown that there is good reason to think that Jesus meant to announce the Jubilee. Sloan uses an important Qumran text (from the Dead Sea Scrolls) that comes from roughly the same time as Jesus. This Qumran text links the Jubilee passage of Leviticus 25 and the Sabbatical release of debts of Deuteronomy 15 with Isaiah 61:1, which Jesus quotes. Furthermore, it gives Isaiah 61:1 a specific Jubilee interpretation. Equally important, all three texts are placed in an eschatological perspective. Thus the Qumran text expects the economic and social reordering described in Leviticus 25, Deuteronomy 15, and Isaiah 61 to occur when the Messiah ushers in the Messianic Age. In fact, Sloan has discovered that in Jewish literature, the Jubilee text is almost always placed in an eschatological context. Luke 4:16–19 would seem to demand a similar interpretation. This means that right at the heart of Jesus' conception of the Messianic Age was the special concern for the poor, the release of captives, and liberation of the oppressed called for in the Jubilee. The New Age that he saw himself inaugurating had specific economic and social content.

Jesus' cleansing of the temple fits perfectly into this inauguration of the Messianic Jubilee. Outraged that the wealthy priestly rulers were collecting huge sums since they had a monopoly on the sale of animals for sacrifice, Jesus called their economic practices robbery ("My house will be a house of prayer, but you have made it a den of robbers"—Luke 19:46). And he drove them out. This was not an armed attack on the Temple. But it was a dramatic act of civil disobedience designed to protest the economic oppression and the desecration of the Temple going on there. It is hardly surprising that the Sadducees and priestly aristocracy considered a person who announced and acted out such a radical call for socioeconomic change to be highly dangerous. One reason Jesus got crucified, then, was that he began to live out the kind of fundamental socioeconomic reordering expected when the Messiah would inaugurate the Jubilee.

Jesus and his new community of followers challenged the status quo at every point that it was wrong—its unmerciful legalism, its dominating leadership, its violence, its oppression of women, and its economic injustice. Jesus and his new society of disciples formed a new kind of society where all broken relationships, whether social, emotional, economic, or spiritual, were being redeemed. The fact that such a new society was now present for people to enter was a central part of what Jesus meant by his announcement of the gospel of the kingdom.

Nor did the early church abandon Jesus' method and message. Through the power of the Holy Spirit the early church was also a strikingly different society where all the Old Age's sinful dividing walls of hostility were being broken down. Jews accepted Gentiles. Slaves and women became persons. Those with financial resources shared generously with anyone in need even if that meant, as in Jerusalem, selling property. The early church was such a strikingly different kind of social order that Paul could say in Galatians 3:28: "There is neither Jew nor Gentile, neither slave nor free, nor is there male and female, for you are all one in Christ Jesus."

Ephesians 3 shows that the fact of this new community where all relationships were being redeemed was part of the content of the gospel Paul proclaimed. In Ephesians 2, Paul had shown how at the cross Jesus had broken through the hostile dividing wall separating Jews and Gentiles, thus creating one new person, one new visible body of Gentile and Jewish believers (2:13–16). Now in chapter 3, Paul proceeds to show that his special mission has been to make known the mystery of Christ. What is the mystery of Christ? Verse 6 demonstrates that the mystery Paul preaches is precisely the fact of the new multi-ethnic body of believers: "This mystery is that through the gospel the Gentiles are heirs together with Israel, members together of one body, and sharers together in the promise in Christ Jesus." The fact that a new, visible community now exists because of the cross where ethnic (as well as cultural, gender, etc.)

hostilities are already overcome is a fundamental part of the gospel. Whenever believers actually dare to live that way, Jesus' new multi-ethnic church is part of the gospel. It is a visible model of the new kingdom Jesus announced.

Thus far we have seen that the gospel we proclaim is the Good News of the kingdom. We have looked at the horizontal dimensions of that message, seeing how the church is a new society where all relationships, whether social, emotional, or economic, are being redeemed. But there are also extremely important vertical dimensions. For the kingdom has a King. And that King is the incarnate Son, Jesus the Christ, who is our Savior and Lord.

Any discussion of the gospel that neglects the glorious Good News that Jesus is our Savior is heretical. Jesus gently accepted sinners, offering them God's unmerited forgiveness. And then he died on the cross as a ransom for our sins. At the heart of the gospel that St. Paul preached throughout the Roman empire was the free offer of justification by faith alone through Christ's atoning death on the cross. Nor does our Savior merely forgive our sins. He also sends the Holy Spirit to blow through our twisted personalities, regenerating, sanctifying, and transforming us into his own image. The head of the kingdom we proclaim is the Savior who forgives and transforms us miserable sinners. That too is absolutely central to the gospel.

But Jesus is not only Savior. As the SACLA theme song reminds us, he is also Lord—Lord of all things in heaven and earth. Paul reminded the Corinthians that the gospel he preached is that Jesus is Lord: "For what we preach is not ourselves, but Jesus Christ as Lord" (2 Corinthians 4:3–5; cf. also Romans 10:8–16 and Phil. 2:9–11).

Seldom, however, do we live out the full implication of the fact that Jesus' Lordship is a fundamental part of the gospel. Positively, the fact that Jesus is Lord means that nothing else can lord it over and dominate our lives. We are liberated from ancient religious taboos, from parental dreams, from oppressive social patterns, from the principalities and powers. Jesus, not Caesar, is Lord. Jesus not Chairman Brezhnev, not President Carter, not Prime Minister

Botha, is Lord. We need not fear disobeying any other person or society for the sake of truth and justice because Jesus alone is absolute Lord. That is exhilarating, liberating Good News.

But there is another side to this aspect of the gospel. If Jesus' Lordship is a fundamental aspect of the gospel, then the call to that unconditional discipleship that this Lord demands is absolutely inseparable from the summons to accept the gospel. Acceptance of costly, unconditional discipleship dare not be an optional second stage separated from acceptance of the gospel.

Jesus repeatedly and pointedly emphasized the cost of discipleship to those who were contemplating becoming his followers.

> Large crowds were traveling with Jesus, and turning to them he said: "If anyone comes to me and does not hate father and mother, wife and children, brothers and sisters—yes, even their own life—such a person cannot be my disciple. And whoever does not carry their cross and follow me cannot be my disciple.
>
> Suppose one of you wants to build a tower. Won't you first sit down and estimate the cost to see if you have enough money to complete it?" (Luke 14:25–28)

In another statement, Jesus makes it clear that a costly commitment to unconditional discipleship is necessarily and inevitably linked to the appropriation of the saving gospel:

> Then he called the crowd to him along with his disciples and said: "Whoever wants to be my disciple must deny themselves and take up their cross and follow me. For whoever wants to save their life will lose it, but whoever loses their life for me and for the gospel will save it." (Mark 8:34–35; cf. also 10:29)

Jesus' encounter with the rich young man (Mark 10:17–31) shows that he never hesitated to emphasize the demands of discipleship. It is simply un-biblical to present only that part of the gospel that corresponds to a person's felt needs. If we present the gospel to, say, a businessman who yearns for forgiveness from the guilt he feels for sexual infidelity, we dare not fail to point out that accepting Jesus' forgiveness will also necessarily include repentance from involvement in sinful economic structures and institutionalized racism. You cannot accept one half of Jesus and reject the other half. You cannot accept the Savior's forgiveness and turn your back on him as Lord of your racial attitudes and business practices.

The gospel is inseparable from costly discipleship. The one who justifies and regenerates also demands that we forsake all other lords and live a transformed lifestyle after the pattern of his perfect life. Accepting Christ as Savior necessarily includes accepting Jesus as Lord of our personal lives, our family life, our racial attitudes, our economics, and our politics. Jesus will not be our Savior if we persistently reject him as our Lord.

That does not mean, of course, that genuine Christians live perfectly surrendered, sinless lives. We continue to be justified by grace alone in spite of ongoing sin. But it does mean that conscious, persistent rejection of Jesus' Lordship in any area of our lives is, as John Calvin taught, a clear sign that saving faith is not present.

Too often Christians (especially evangelical Protestants in recent times) have proclaimed a cheap grace that offers the forgiveness of the gospel without the discipleship demands of the gospel. But that is not Jesus' gospel. There is only one biblical gospel. And that is the Good News about one whose demand for submission to his Lordship is as total and unconditional as his mercy is free and unmerited. Since Jesus' Lordship is a central aspect of the gospel, the summons to costly discipleship is inseparable from biblically sound evangelism.

What is evangelism? It is sharing the glorious Good News that the kingdom of God has become powerfully present and visibly victorious in the person and work of Jesus Christ. It is announcing the astonishing message that God accepts sinners just as they are and enters into a personal, living relationship with them because of the Savior's death. It is communicating the solid assurance that because Jesus is Lord, no other lords and masters, whether human or demonic, can ever lord it over us and terrorize us anymore.

What an utterly fantastic message! Every person in our gloriously created, tragically broken world needs to hear it. Those who are overwhelmed with guilty consciences long for the forgiveness our message brings. Those who feel that life is meaningless or hopeless yearn for the solid hope that comes from knowing that the Risen Jesus has won the decisive victory over sin, injustice, and death and that he will complete that victory at his second coming. Those who are battered and broken by the inhumanity and oppression of the world cry and weep for Jesus' new community of followers. Jesus intends the church to be a visible model of what heaven will be like.

The early church was that—it was a radically new kind of society where the broken and the strong, the poor and the rich, the oppressed and the oppressors confessed their sins, and shared their resources, letting the Holy Spirit create one, new, redeemed society where all things were being made new. And in the course of a few short centuries, they spread like wildfire and overturned the Roman Empire. I am absolutely certain that God will do the same in our day if we dare to preach and live this whole biblical gospel.

The second part of my presentation deals with the question of social justice. Both Old and New Testaments summon God's people to be concerned for justice. "Let justice roll down like waters" is the constant theme of the prophets. Jesus condemned the scribes and Pharisees in Matthew 23:23 for their preoccupation with tithing and their neglect of weightier matters of the law such as mercy and justice.

The field is so vast that I must be very selective. I want to focus on two issues:

1. The Bible teaches that participation in structural injustice or systemic evil is just as sinful as committing personal sinful acts like lying or adultery;

2. One of the central biblical doctrines is that God is on the side of the poor and oppressed.

First the question of structural injustice or systemic evil. Let me illustrate what I mean with a story from my hometown of Philadelphia.

In the early 1950s, Northeast High School in Philadelphia was famous for its superb academic standards and its brilliant, long-standing athletic triumphs. The second oldest school in the city, Northeast had excellent teachers and a great tradition. And it was almost entirely white. Then in the mid-fifties, the neighborhood began to change. Black people moved in. Whites began to flee in droves to the Greater Northeast, a new, all-white section of Philadelphia. Quite naturally, a new high school became necessary much farther out in this developing, overwhelmingly white area.

When the excellent new school was completed in 1957, the new school took along the name, Northeast High School, with its fond memories and traditions and many connotations of academic excellence and athletic triumph. The inner-city school was renamed Edison High. The new school took all the academic and athletic trophies and awards, school colors and songs, powerful alumni and all the money in the treasury. Worst of all, the teachers were given the option of transferring to the new Northeast High. Two-thirds of them did.

The black students who now attended Edison High had an old, rapidly deteriorating building, frequent substitute teachers, and no traditions. Nor did the intervening years bring many better teachers or adequate teaching materials. The academic record since 1957 has been terrible. In fact Edison High has only one claim to uniqueness. It has one national record. More students from Edison High died in the United States army in Vietnam than from any other high school in the United States!

Who was guilty of this terrible sin? Local, state, and federal politicians who had promoted de facto housing segregation for decades? The school board? Parents who had, at best, a very partial picture of what was going on? Christian community leaders? The white high school students at the new Northeast High whose excellent education and future job prospects have been possible, in part, precisely because of the poor facilities and bad teachers left behind for the black students at Edison? Who was guilty?

Many would deny any personal responsibility. "That's just the way things are." And they would be quite right! Long-standing patterns in jobs and housing had created a system that automatically produced Edison High. But that hardly silences the question about responsibility. Do we sin when we participate in evil social systems and societal structures that unfairly benefit some and harm others?

Neglect of the biblical teaching on structural injustice or institutionalized evil is one of the most deadly omissions in some segments of the church today.

There is an important difference between consciously willed individual acts like, say, lying to a friend or committing an act of adultery, and participation in evil social structures. Slavery is an example of an institutionalized evil. So is the Victorian factory system where ten-year-old children worked twelve to sixteen hours a day. Both were perfectly legal, but they destroyed millions of people. They were institutionalized or structural evils.

Some Christians today seem primarily preoccupied with personal sins, others seem to care about only evil structures. But the Bible cares about both. Speaking through his prophet Amos, the Lord declares, "For three transgressions of Israel, even for four, I will not relent." Why? Because "they sell the innocent for silver, and the needy for a pair of sandals. They trample on the heads of the poor as on the dust of the ground, and deny justice to the oppressed." Thus far the text is talking about oppression of the poor but it goes on, and says God will also punish them because "father and son use the same girl and so profane my holy name" (Amos 2:6–7).

Two things are important here. Biblical scholars have shown that some kind of legal fiction underlies the phrase "selling the needy for a pair of sandals." This mistreatment of the poor was legal. Notice too that God condemns both sexual misconduct and legalized oppression of the poor. Sexual sins and economic injustice are equally displeasing to the God of Scripture.

God revealed the same thing through his prophet Isaiah:

> Woe to you who add house to house
> and join field to field

till no space is left

and you live alone in the land.

The Lord Almighty has declared in my hearing:

"Surely the great houses will become desolate,

the fine mansions left without occupants" . . .

Woe to those who rise early in the morning

to run after their drinks,

who stay up late at night

till they are inflamed with wine. (Isaiah 5:8–11).

Here God condemns both the wealthy who amass large land-holdings at the expense of the poor and also those who have fallen into drunkenness. Great economic inequality is just as abominable to our just God as drunkenness.

One of the tragedies of our time is that some young activists have supposed that as long as they were fighting for social justice, they were morally righteous regardless of how often they went to bed for the night with a girl or guy in the movement. Some of their elders, on the other hand, have supposed that because they do not lie, steal, and fornicate, they are morally upright even though they silently support institutionalized racism and own stock in companies that exploit the poor of the earth. God, however, has shown that robbing one's workers of a fair wage is just as sinful as robbing a bank. Voting for a racist because he is a racist is just as sinful as sleeping with your neighbor's wife!

God also shows that laws themselves are sometimes an abomination to him. Listen to Psalm 94:20–23: "Can a corrupt throne be allied with you—a throne that brings on misery by its decrees? The wicked band together against the righteous and condemn the innocent to death. But the Lord has become my fortress, and my God the rock in whom I take refuge. He will repay them for their sins and destroy them for their wickedness; the Lord our God will destroy them." The Jerusalem Bible has an excellent rendition of verse 20. It says, "You never consent [that is, you never should consent] to that corrupt tribunal that imposes disorder as law." God wants his people to know that wicked governments sometimes frame mischief by statute. Or as the New English Bible puts it, "They contrive evil under cover of law." God proclaims the same word through the prophet Isaiah: "Woe to those who make unjust laws and those who issue oppressive decrees." Why do they do that? "To deprive the poor of their rights and withhold justice from the oppressed of my people" (Isaiah 10:1–4). It's quite possible to wreak oppression legally. But legalized oppression is an abomination to God, and therefore God commands God's people to oppose it.

There is one other side to social or institutionalized evil that makes it especially pernicious. Social evil is so subtle that one can be caught in it without realizing it. God inspired his prophet Amos to utter some of the harshest words in Scripture against the cultured, kind, upper-class women of his day. "Hear this word, you cows of Bashan on Mount Samaria, you women who oppress the poor and crush the needy and say to your husbands, 'Bring us some drinks!' The Sovereign Lord has sworn by his holiness: 'The time will surely come when you will be taken away with hooks, the last of you with fishhooks'" (Amos 4:1–2). Now the women involved probably had no contact or very little contact with the impoverished peasants. They may never have realized clearly that their gorgeous clothes and spirited parties were possible only because of the sweat and tears of toiling peasants. In fact they may even have been kind to individual peasants that they met. Perhaps they gave them "Christmas baskets" once a year. But God called these privileged ladies "cows" because they profited from social evil. Hence, they were personally and individually guilty before God.

Surely this text teaches that if one is a member of a privileged class that profits from an unjust system, and if one is not working hard to change it, then one stands guilty before God. Social evil or structural injustice is just as sinful as personal sin, and it often hurts more people. And it's a lot more subtle.

The second biblical teaching related to the question of justice is God's special concern for the poor and oppressed. There are literally hundreds of verses in the Bible that say that God has a very special concern for the poor and oppressed. I think the best way to summarizing these verses is to say that God is on the side of the poor.

Now please do not misunderstand me at this point. I do *not* mean that God loves the poor more than the rich. I do *not* mean that the poor and oppressed are saved just because they are poor and oppressed. The poor must repent of their sins and enter into a living personal relationship with the risen Lord Jesus in the same way as white middle-class sinners do if they are to be saved. Finally, I do *not* mean that God is a Marxist and that we should read a Marxist ideology into the Bible.

But the Bible does say two very pointed things that I think are best summarized by saying God is on the side of the poor and oppressed:

1. God is at work in history casting down the unjust rich and exalting the poor and oppressed;

2. The people of God, if they are really the people of God, are also on the side of the poor.

Before I develop these two points, I want to tell you about a long talk I had recently with the head of a large evangelical agency. We were talking about poverty and injustice and about what the Bible has to say about God's special concern with the poor. After a while, this fifty-year-old evangelical leader looked me in the eye and asked with sad perplexity: "How could I grow up as a Bible-believing evangelical, study and then teach at a thoroughly evangelical college and seminary and never come to see until last year that the Bible clearly teaches that God is on the side of the poor?"

Let's look at what the Bible says.

The first element of the biblical teaching that God is on the side of the poor and oppressed is that the Bible says that God acts in history to exalt the poor and to cast down the rich. Mary's Magnificat puts it bluntly: "My soul glorifies the Lord . . . He has brought down rulers from their thrones, but has lifted up the humble. He has filled the hungry with good things, but has sent the rich away empty" (Luke 1:47–53). The text in James 5:1 says: "Now listen, you rich people, weep and wail because of the misery that is coming on you." That is a constant theme of biblical revelation.

Now why does Scripture declare that God regularly reverses the good fortunes of the rich? Precisely because the wealthy have often become rich by oppressing the poor or because they have failed to aid the needy. Why did James warn the rich to weep and howl? Because they had oppressed their workers. James 5:3–5 says: "You have hoarded wealth in the last days. Look! The wages you failed to pay the workers who mowed your fields are crying out against you. The cries of the harvesters have reached the ears of the Lord Almighty. You have lived on earth in luxury and self-indulgence. You have fattened yourselves in the day of slaughter." So James. God does not have class enemies. But God hates and God punishes injustice and neglect of the poor and oppressed. And the rich, if we listen to Scripture, are frequently guilty of both.

Long before the days of James, Jeremiah knew that the rich were often rich because of oppression. Listen to Jeremiah 5:26–28: "Among my people are the wicked who lie in wait like men who snare birds and like those who set traps to catch people. Like cages full of birds, their houses are full of deceit; they have become rich and powerful and have grown fat and sleek. Their evil deeds have no limit; they do not seek justice. They do not promote the case of the fatherless; they do not defend the just cause of the poor. 'Should I not punish them for this?' declares the Lord." Through the prophets God announced devastating destruction for both rich individuals and rich nations who oppressed the poor.

One more example in Isaiah 3:14–15: "The Lord enters into judgment against the elders and leaders of his people: 'It is you who have ruined my vineyard, the plunder from the poor is in your houses. What do you mean by crushing my people, by grinding the faces of the poor?' declares the Lord Almighty." Because the rich oppress the poor and the weak, the Lord of history, Scripture says, is at work pulling down their houses and their societies.

Now sometimes Scripture does not accuse the rich of direct oppression of the poor. It simply accuses them of failure to aid and share with the needy. But the result is the same. The biblical explanation of Sodom's destruction is one example. Through the prophet Ezekiel God says that one important reason that God destroyed Sodom was that she stubbornly refused to share with the poor. Ezekiel 16:48–50 reads: "Behold this was the sin of your sister Sodom: She and her daughters were arrogant, overfed, and unconcerned; They did not help the poor and needy . . . therefore I did away with them." The text doesn't say they oppressed the poor, although perhaps they did. It simply says that they failed to aid the needy. According to the Bible, God is at work in history casting down the unjust rich and powerful. Why? Because they often get rich by oppressing the poor or they fail to aid the needy.

The second part of the biblical teaching that God is on the side of the poor is that the people of God, if they are really the people of God, are also on the side of the poor. It seems to me that God's word clearly teaches that those who neglect the poor and the oppressed are really not God's people at all, no matter how frequent their religious rituals or how orthodox their creeds and their confessions.

The prophets sometimes made this point by insisting that knowledge of God and seeking justice for the oppressed are inseparable. At other times they condemned the religious rituals of the oppressors who tried to worship God and still continue to oppress the poor.

Jeremiah announced God's harsh message that King Jehoiakim, a very oppressive, unjust king, did not know Jahweh and would be destroyed because of his injustice:

> Woe to him who builds his palace by unrighteousness,
>> his upper rooms by injustice,
> making his own people work for nothing
>> not paying them for their labor.
> He says, "I will build myself a great palace
>> with spacious upper rooms."
> So he makes large windows in it,
>> panels it with cedar

and decorates it in red.

Does it make you a king

to have more and more cedar?

Did not your father have food and drink?

He did what was right and just,

so all went well with him.

He defended the cause of the poor and needy,

and so all went well.

Is that not what it means to know me?

declares the Lord. (Jeremiah 22:13–16)

Knowing God necessarily involves seeking justice for the poor and needy (cf. also Hosea 2:19–20).

Some theologians of liberation distort this biblical truth and wrongly say that knowing God is nothing more than seeking justice for the oppressed. That is an unbiblical humanism. To liberation theologians like Jose Miranda, we must insist that knowing God involves a lot more than seeking justice for the oppressed. But to some evangelical Christians who prefer to forget about the call to justice, we must insist equally strongly that knowing God dare not involve less than costly commitment to the search for social justice.

The prophets said this again and again by announcing God's outrage against worship in the context of mistreatment of the poor and disadvantaged. God abhors those who mix worship and oppression. Isaiah denounced Israel (he called her Sodom and Gomorrah) because she tried to worship Jahweh and oppress the weak at the same time (Isaiah 1:10–17).

Is not this the kind of fasting I have chosen:

to loose the chains of injustice

and untie the cords of the yoke,

to set the oppressed free

and break every yoke?

Is it not to share your food with the hungry

and to provide the poor wanderer with shelter—

when you see the naked, to clothe them,

and not to turn away from your own flesh

and blood? (Isaiah 58:3–7; likewise Isaiah 1:10–17)

God's words through the prophet Amos are also harsh:

I hate, I despise your religious festivals;

your assemblies are a stench to me.

Even though you bring me burnt offerings

and grain offerings,

I will not accept them . . .

But let justice roll on like a river,

righteousness like a never-failing stream! (Amos
5:21–24)

Earlier in the chapter, Amos had condemned the rich and powerful for oppressing the poor. They even bribed judges to prevent redress in the courts. God wants justice, not mere religious rituals, from God's people. Worship mixed with economic oppression is a mockery and abomination to the God of the poor.

Nor has God changed. Jesus repeated the same theme. He warned the people about scribes who secretly oppress widows while making a public display of their piety. Their pious-looking garments and frequent visits to the synagogue were a sham, he said.

Now Jesus' and the prophets' warning against religious hypocrites raises an extremely difficult question for us. Are the people of God really the people of God at all if they oppress the poor? Is the church really the church at all if it doesn't work to free the oppressed?

Through the prophets God declared that the people of Israel were actually Sodom and Gomorrah rather than God's people because of their exploitation of the poor and the weak. Jesus was even more blunt and more sharp. To those who do not feed the hungry and clothe the naked, he will speak the word at the final judgment: "Depart from me, you who are cursed, into the eternal fire prepared for the devil and his angels" (Matthew 25:4). The meaning is clear and unambiguous. Jesus intends his disciples to imitate his own special concern for the poor and the oppressed. Those who disobey will experience eternal damnation.

And lest we forget that warning, God repeats it in 1 John 3:17: "If anyone has material possessions and sees a brother or a sister in need, but has not pity on them, how can the love of God be in that person?" Again the words are plain, but what do they mean for affluent Christians who enjoy their luxurious lifestyle while others suffer malnutrition and oppression? The text clearly says that if we fail to aid the needy, we don't have God's love, no matter what we say. This text demands deeds, not pious phrases and saintly speeches. Regardless of what creeds we confess or what religious experience we claim, affluent people who neglect the poor and oppressed are not the people of God at all. That's what Scripture says.

But still the question haunts me. Are professing believers no longer Christians because of continuing sin? Obviously not. The Christian knows that sinful selfishness continues to plague even the most saintly. We are members of the people of God not because of our good works but solely because of Christ's death for us.

That response is extremely important and very true. But it is also inadequate. All the texts from both testaments that we have just surveyed surely mean more than that the people of God are disobedient (but still justified all the same) when they neglect the poor. These verses pointedly assert that some people so disobey God that they are not God's people at all, in spite of their pious profession. Neglect of the poor is one of the oft-repeated biblical signs of such disobedience. Certainly none of us would claim that we fulfill Matthew 25 perfectly. And we cling to the hope of forgiveness. But there comes a point—and, thank God, God alone knows where!—when neglect of the poor is no longer forgiven. It is punished. Eternally.

In light of these two clear biblical truths about systemic injustice and God on the side of the poor and oppressed, how biblical is our theology today? I'm afraid that most white Christians must confess that they are largely on the side of the rich oppressors rather than the oppressed poor. Imagine what would happen if all Christian institutions—our youth organizations, our publications, our seminaries, our congregations, and denominational head-quarters—would all dare to undertake a comprehensive, two-year examination of their total program and activity to answer this question: Is there the same balance and emphasis on structural evil and justice for the poor and oppressed in our programs as there is in Scripture? I am willing to predict that if one quarter of those who call themselves evangelicals would do that with an unconditional readiness to change whatever did not correspond with the biblical revelation of God's special concern for the poor and oppressed, we would unleash a biblical movement of social justice that would change the course of modern history.

But our problem is not primarily one of ethics. It is not that we have failed to live what our teachers have taught. Our theology itself has been unbiblical and therefore heretical. By largely ignoring the central biblical teaching that God is on the side of the poor, evangelical theology has been profoundly unorthodox. The Bible has just as much to say about this doctrine as it does about Jesus' resurrection. And yet we insist (rightly, I believe) on the resurrection as a criterion of orthodoxy and largely ignore the equally prominent biblical teaching that God is on the side of the poor and the oppressed.

Now please do not misunderstand me at this point. I am not saying that the resurrection is unimportant. The bodily resurrection of Jesus of Nazareth is absolutely central to Christian faith and any-one who denies it or says it is unimportant has fallen into heresy. But if centrality in Scripture is any criterion of doctrinal importance, then the biblical teaching that God is on the side of the poor ought to be an extremely important doctrine for Christians.

I am afraid we evangelical Christians have fallen into theological liberalism.

Of course we usually think of theological liberalism in terms of classical nineteenth-century liberals who denied the deity, the atonement, and the bodily resurrection of Jesus our Lord. And that is correct. People who abandon those central biblical doctrines have fallen into terrible heresy. But notice what the essence of theological liberalism is—it is allowing our thinking and living to be shaped by surrounding society's views and values rather than by biblical revelation. Liberal theologians thought that belief in the deity of Jesus Christ and his bodily resurrection was incompatible with a modern scientific worldview. So they followed surrounding "scientific" society rather than Scripture.

Evangelicals rightly called attention to this heresy—and then tragically made exactly the same move in another area. We have allowed the values of our affluent, unjust society to shape our thinking and acting toward the poor and oppressed. It is much easier in evangelical circles today to insist on an orthodox Christology than to insist on the biblical teaching that God abhors unjust social systems and that God is on the side of the poor and oppressed. We have allowed our theology to be shaped by our sinful, unjust societies rather than by Scripture. And that is to fall into theological liberalism. We have not been nearly as orthodox as we have claimed.

Past failure, however, is no reason for despair. I think we mean it when we sing, "I'd rather have Jesus than houses or lands." I think we mean it when we write and affirm doctrinal statements that boldly declare that we will not only believe but also live whatever Scripture teaches. But if we do mean it, then we must teach and live in a world full of injustice, oppression, and starvation, the important biblical doctrines that God wills justice in society and that God and God's faithful people are on the side of the poor and oppressed. Unless we drastically reshape both our theology and our entire institutional church life so that the fact that God is on the side of the poor and oppressed becomes as central to our theology and institutional programs as it is in Scripture, we will demonstrate to the world that our verbal commitment to *sola scriptura* is a dishonest ideological support for an unjust, oppressive status quo. But I hope and believe that in the next few years, millions of biblical Christians in every country in the world will allow the scriptural teaching that God is on the side of the poor and oppressed to fundamentally reshape our culturally conditioned theology and our unbiblically one-sided programs and institutions. If that happens, God will use the contemporary church, as he once used the early church, to change the course of world history.

I have tried to develop a biblical perspective on both evangelism and the search for justice. Let me conclude with a few comments on their relationship. Evangelism and social action are not identical. Working to end social injustice is not the same as inviting someone to accept Christ as personal Lord and Savior. Evangelism and social action must not be confused with each other although they are inextricably interrelated.

Let me note several aspects of their interrelationship.

In the first place, proclamation of the biblical gospel necessarily includes a call to repentance and turning away from all forms of sin. Sin is both personal and structural. Evangelicals regularly preach that coming to Jesus means forsaking adultery, lying, and stealing. Too often, however, they fail to add that coming to Jesus necessarily involves repentance of and conversion from the sin of involvement in structural evils such as economic injustice and institutionalized racism. Biblical evangelism will call for repentance of one's involvement in both individual and structural sins. And since the gospel also includes the proclamation of Jesus' total Lordship, biblical evangelism will clearly declare the cost of unconditional discipleship. Accepting Christ as Savior means accepting him as Lord of every area of one's life.

Second, simply living the full New Testament reality of the church frequently constitutes a challenge to the status quo. Think of what would happen if all the Christians in South Africa truly began to care for each other and share their time, their money, and their lives with each other across racial and economic lines the way the early church did. Nothing would be more revolutionary than simply living out day by day the full biblical teaching that in Christ there is neither Jew nor Greek, black nor white, because we are all one in Christ. The South African church has the fantastic opportunity to offer to society a visible model of the way people can live together in more loving and just ways. Simply living a new model in defiance of the norms and accepted values of surrounding society would powerfully affect the total social order.

Third, seeking justice sometimes facilitates the task of evangelism. Just as the very oppressed situation of persons trapped in unjust social structures sometimes hinders a positive response to the gospel, so too increasing social justice may make some people more open to the Good News. Sometimes precisely the act of working in the name of Jesus for improved socioeconomic conditions for the oppressed enables persons to understand the proclaimed word of God's love in Christ. In that situation, the act of social concern is itself truly evangelistic. Furthermore, a biblically informed social action will not fail to point out that participation in social injustice is not just inhuman behavior toward neighbor but also damnable sin against Almighty God. Hence biblical social action will contain, always implicitly and often explicitly, a call to repentance.

In practice then, evangelism and the search for justice are intricately interrelated. They are inseparable both in the sense that evangelism often leads to increased social justice and vice versa and also that biblical Christians will, precisely to the extent that they are faithful followers of Jesus, always seek liberty for the oppressed (Luke 4:18).

Does the church today have the courage to witness in both words and deeds to the biblical God who calls his people to both evangelism and the search for justice? That will take courage and commitment in all continents and countries. Nowhere will it take more faith and courage than here. The task seems overwhelming and impossible. But biblical Christians have done it in the past and they can do it again.

William Wilberforce and his small band of evangelical Christians worked for thirty years to end the slave trade and then slavery itself. They changed the course of British history.

Charles Finney and his band of American abolitionists working to abolish slavery were equally evangelical. Finney was the Billy Graham of the nineteenth century. He led evangelistic crusades throughout the country. The filling of the Holy Spirit was central in his life and preaching. He was also one of the leading abolitionists working to end the unjust system of slavery. Church discipline was used at his church at Oberlin College, which he founded, against anyone holding slaves. Finney and his students practiced civil disobedience to protest unjust laws. Over Christmas holidays, Finney's students went out by the scores to hold evangelistic meetings. And they preached against the sin of participating in slavery as well as personal sins. Historians have shown that the abolitionist movement in many states of the Midwest in the United States grew directly out of these revival campaigns by Finney and his students.

I dream of that kind of movement in the church today: a movement that is filled with the Holy Spirit; a movement that immerses its activity in prayer; a movement that declares the gospel to every person who has not yet accepted Jesus Christ as personal Lord and Savior; a movement that challenges every injustice in society in the name of the God revealed in Holy Scripture.

I dream of a biblically balanced church that will go to every person no matter how poor and oppressed, no matter how battered and trampled their self-esteem and initiative may be, and tell them that the Lord of this whole universe loves them. A church that will tell them that God wants them to repent of their despair and sin and enter into a living personal relationship with the risen Lord of history. I dream of a biblical church that will be visibly demonstrating in its common life such different, loving, redeemed relationships that the poor and oppressed will flock to their fellowship. Such a church will hasten to share the biblical truth that the God who now lives in their hearts is a God of justice who abhors present unjust social systems that discriminate and oppress. Nothing could be more revolutionary in a peaceful way than a faithful sharing of this total biblical truth with the poor and oppressed.

I dream of a church that will dare to go to the rich and powerful and tell them that God loves them too and wants them to repent and follow Christ. Certainly such a church would never forget to say that they must accept Jesus as Lord as well as Savior, that coming to Christ means not just forgiveness of sins but radical change so that Christ is Lord of all business practices and political decisions regardless of the cost.

I dream of a church that would immerse all of this activity in deep, intercessory prayer, a church that is totally dependent on the transforming breath of the blessed Holy Spirit. I dream of a church that would have tens of thousands of persons interceding all night as others approached officials in government and business to call for sweeping systemic changes for the sake of justice. I dream of a church whose members are politically active for the sake of the justice God wills.

I dream of a church that would, after it had exhausted every other available means for influencing government, even dare to use massive boycotts and civil disobedience to demand an end to injustice. I dream of a church that remembers that earlier heroes of the faith defied government knowing they had to obey God rather than men, a church that as a last resort peacefully and prayerfully in the power of the Holy Spirit embarks on total non-cooperation with governments until they seek justice and correct oppression.

Such a church would be persecuted like the early Christians. Such a church would have martyrs. Such a church might also change the course of world history.

Is there any other choice? Will anything less be adequate at this late date? Dare those who confess Jesus as personal Lord and Savior, those who know that he is the Risen Sovereign of history, do any less?

I want to end by sharing a recent experience that profoundly moved me. I talked a few days ago with a prominent Dutch Reformed Christian. As many, many others have, he too expressed his despair that peaceful change could come. He said he feared the chances were very high that his beloved country would drift into a bloody civil war that would kill tens of thousands. He seemed to have no hope.

I said to him, "What would happen if 10,000 biblical Christians committed to God and each other began to pray and intercede with God day after day, week after week, seeking the guidance of the Holy Spirit? And then, after they had begun to live what it means to be the church among themselves, and when God said go, they would go prayerfully and peacefully to government and say: 'We come in the name of the risen Jesus. He alone is our Lord. You also confess him as Lord. In the name of the God of the Bible, we say the present injustice must end. Now! It dare not go on another five years or ten years. God has told us to stay here and pray until it changes, regardless of the cost.'"

The Dutch Reformed Christian responded: "That would change everything. If a group of white, Bible-believing Christians went peacefully in that way, the government would have to respond."

Then he added: "You would not need 10,000." "Would 5,000 be enough?," I asked. He said: "You would not need that many." I thought: "Oh my God, are there not 3,000 Christians who will bear any cross to stand in that gap? When the alternative is a ghastly war that will kill tens of thousands, are there not 3,000 Christians ready to risk even their lives for peace and justice?"

I end with the words of 1 Peter 2:21: "To this you were called, because Christ suffered for you, leaving you an example, that you should follow in his steps."

Chapter 8: Why Are We Buying the New Property?

[I preached this sermon at my church, Oxford Circle Mennonite Church in Philadelphia, on November 16, 2008, as our small congregation with fewer than fifty members was in the audacious process of purchasing a large $3.5 million property so we could greatly expand our holistic community development work in the surrounding neighborhood.]

WHY ARE WE BUYING the new property? The simple answer to the question is this: People need Jesus and they need a job. People have both spiritual and material needs. People have bodies as well as souls. That is why people need Jesus and a job.

That's the answer to my question: Why are we buying the new property? So I guess I could stop there. But you probably expect the sermon to be a little longer.

Two stories about dear friends illustrate my point that people need Jesus and a job.

John Perkins grew up in a poor black community in rural Mississippi. After his older brother was killed by a white racist, Perkins moved to California where he got a good job. Then his oldest son started going to a Sunday school and when John visited the church, John met Christ. Soon John felt called to return to poor, rural Mississippi and share the gospel there. As young people began to come to Christ in his Bible studies for local high school students, Perkins realized they also needed tutoring and health-care and decent jobs. So he started helping students prepare for college, began a health clinic, and started a store to provide jobs and good products.

This holistic model of community development in poor communities—where Christians both invite persons to Christ and also minister to all their socioeconomic needs—has spread to hundreds of poor neighborhoods. Every year, thousands of people attend the annual conference of the Christian Community Development Association, which John Perkins started to spread the vision of holistic ministry.

A second story illustrates the same point. For many years, Glen Kehrein and Raleigh Washington have led a large holistic program similar to the John Perkins model in a poor section of Chicago. They do job training, run a huge medical clinic, provide legal services, and many other things, helping to transform a large community. But they also invite people to accept Christ and many hundreds have.

Wanda Caldwell first came to their program as a teenager needing medical care. The doctor prayed with her before he did a needed operation. But she returned to the streets for ten years, abusing alcohol and drugs and collecting welfare. Finally, at a desperately low situation in her life, Wanda returned to the church that met in the gym of the large community center program. She soon accepted Christ and the community center's medical and legal programs provided assistance as Christ and Christ's people transformed her life.

If Wanda had come to some of our church programs, she would have received an invitation to accept Christ but no help with her physical, material needs. If she had come to some different church programs, she would have received a bag of groceries and a tract on how to lobby government, but no word about her need for Christ. Thank God Wanda came to a Christian ministry that knew that she needed both spiritual and material transformation.

Jesus knew people need both. That's why Jesus said his gospel is the Good News of the kingdom. At the beginning of Mark's Gospel, Mark summarizes Jesus' Good News with the words, "The time is come, the kingdom of God has come near, repent and believe the good news" (Mark 1:14–15).

According to Jesus, the gospel is the Good News of the kingdom. And it's very important to understand the gospel the way Jesus talked about it. Many Christians do not see the importance and the implications of defining the gospel the way Jesus did. Many Christians define the gospel as just the forgiveness of sins so we can go to heaven when we die. But if the gospel is just forgiveness of sins, then it is a one-way ticket to heaven and we can live like hell until we get there. People can accept the gospel and not change at all how they behave. But everything is different if Jesus' gospel is the Good News of the Kingdom. Everything is different if Jesus' gospel includes caring for the poor, freeing prisoners, healing the blind, and freeing the oppressed.

And that is exactly what Jesus says when he announces his mission in Luke 4:18–19:

> The Spirit of the Lord is on me,
> because he has anointed me
> to proclaim good news to the poor.
> He has sent me to proclaim freedom for the prisoners
> and recovery of sight for the blind,
> to set the oppressed free,
> to proclaim the year of the Lord's favor.

When the Old Testament prophets looked ahead to the coming of the Messiah, they said the Messiah would bring both forgiveness of sins in a new way and also bring transformed socioeconomic arrangements. As the Messiah, Jesus brought both.

Forgiveness of sins was certainly at the center of what Jesus announced. In parable after parable, he taught that God longed to forgive prodigal sons and daughters. But Jesus' gospel is much more than just forgiveness of sins. As we saw in Luke 4, Jesus says his mission is to proclaim good news to the poor. He says he was sent to proclaim freedom for the oppressed and recovery of sight for the blind. He said he was sent to set the oppressed free.

Jesus cared about the whole person. He certainly preached forgiveness of sins. He said we can have a new, wonderful relationship with God in spite of our sin! God is holy. Our God hates sin. God weeps when we hurt other people. Yet Jesus says: "I know sinners are guilty. But God still loves them and I will die in their place. I will suffer their punishment on the cross." Our holy God totally forgives our sins when we repent. No matter how much you have messed up your life, no matter how much you have wronged other people, God still loves you. God longs to forgive you if you just ask God for forgiveness. Jesus took our punishment and now we are totally, completely accepted with God.

That is absolutely wonderful! It is at the very heart of the gospel. But it is only half of Jesus' gospel.

We understand Jesus' gospel as the Good News of the kingdom much better when we remember what the Jews of Jesus day were expecting when the Messiah came. They were expecting a Messiah who would bring peace on earth and justice for the poor.

Jesus says, "That's what I'm doing: feeding the poor, healing the sick, freeing the oppressed, bringing economic justice." Jesus says, "The messianic kingdom you are expecting when everything will be made whole is right now breaking into history in my work as I heal the sick and free the oppressed."

And part of Jesus' proclamation of the gospel of the kingdom was his challenge to an unjust status quo. Jesus challenged the rich to share with the poor. Jesus challenged people's attitudes toward lepers and gently touched them. Jesus challenged people's attitudes toward the blind. Jesus challenged attitudes toward women. Jesus challenged attitudes toward enemies, insisting we should love even them.

Jesus and his new circle of disciples were a living, visible illustration of his gospel of the kingdom. They were a visible demonstration that the messianic kingdom was actually breaking into history.

So you and I, Oxford Circle Mennonite Church, must love the whole person the way Jesus did. We must invite broken people who have messed up their lives and have also been messed up by others to accept Jesus as their personal Lord and Savior. We must invite them to ask Jesus to forgive their sins and embrace the astonishing truth that God no longer sees them as sinners.

But that is only half of the Good News. When people come into a personal relationship with Jesus, they receive not only Jesus' forgiveness but also Jesus's power in their lives. Jesus comes to live in our hearts. Jesus gives us new strength to say no to temptation.

Jesus transforms broken people like Wanda Caldwell. She was living a miserable life that was destroying her. But Jesus entered her heart and life and transformed her. Jesus gives all of us the strength day by day to live more like him.

That is utterly fantastic Good News! People need Jesus—both his forgiveness and his power in their lives. But people also need a job. They need a job that lifts them out of poverty and provides health coverage. They need decent housing and quality education for their children. They need safety and peace on the streets. Jesus' gospel of the kingdom teaches us that Jesus cares about all of that.

And Jesus' church, his body, is the primary way God works out that care for the whole person. That's why this church already runs a summer program for young people with special needs. That's why we have a mentoring program for young students.

That's also why we have all kinds of dreams at Oxford Circle Christian Community Development Association to develop programs in job training, family counseling, college prep mentoring, creation of small businesses, good, modestly priced housing—the possibilities go on and on and on. We care about everything that will help people in Oxford Circle have a good job, wholesome happy families, good housing, and quality education. When we do that, we are living out Jesus' gospel of the kingdom. We are demonstrating by our actions that Jesus' gospel means that justice and peace and wholeness are now breaking into history. Justice for the poor and oppressed is possible now.

But not perfectly. All we have to do is look around, and it is painfully obvious that terrible injustice continues. Violence and war still destroy people by the millions. So does poverty.

So that poses a tough question. If Jesus' gospel is the Good News of the kingdom and that means the time of peace and justice has broken into our history with Jesus and his church, why is there still so much evil around?

Jesus' answer is that his kingdom has already begun but it is not yet complete. Jesus' kingdom has broken into history. The church is supposed to be a little visible picture of what the future will be like when Christ returns. But the church is far from perfect. Only when Christ returns will everything be completely set right.

The Bible says that when Christ comes back to earth the second time, he will complete his victory over all sin, all brokenness, all evil. Romans 8:18–25 tells us that even the groaning creation (the rivers and trees and animals) will be restored to wholeness when Christ returns and you and I are raised bodily from the dead.

Revelation 21 and 22 say that at Christ's return, the new Jerusalem, the perfect city, will come down to earth from heaven. God will dwell with us on this earth in a new way as we are resurrected from the dead. God will wipe every tear from our eyes. The glory of the nations—the best of human civilization, art, and culture—all that will be purged of its evil and taken up into the new Jerusalem. All things will be made new.

We know that is going to happen. We know where history is going. Jesus rose triumphant from the grave and conquered death. He has promised to return sometime in the future and finish the victory over sin, injustice, even death itself.

Because we know that the gospel is the Good News of the kingdom; because we know that the messianic kingdom has already begun to become visible in Jesus' body, the church; because we know that right now broken people no matter how messed up, can accept Jesus' forgiveness and receive divine power in their lives; because of all of that, we invite hurting people to accept Jesus as their personal savior. And we also promise to walk alongside broken people to help them experience the total transformation that they need.

The new building will give us a lot more space to love the whole person, body and soul, the way Jesus did. The new building will help us offer people Jesus and a job.

Dream with me for just a minute as we imagine what God might use this little congregation to do in the next twenty years. Remember what happened in John Perkins's life. It started very small with a few teenagers in a Bible club. As they came to Christ, Perkins's ministry reached out to transform all areas of their lives. The same thing can happen here in Oxford Circle.

I dream that in twenty years, we have a college prep mentoring and tutoring program for high school kids that is sending dozens of young people to college every year.

I dream of a Wholesome Families program that is helping dozens of couples become better mothers and fathers, raising thousands of joyful, flourishing children.

I dream of a welfare to work program that is helping dozens and dozens of single mothers prepare for and succeed at a good job.

I dream of a job training program that prepares scores of our neighbors to find a better job.

I dream of a recovery program that is walking with dozens of hurting people, mentoring them and helping God to transform lives.

I dream of a small business development program that empowers scores of our neighbors to start small businesses , employ a few friends, and greatly expand the income of both their own family and their employees.

I dream of a legal clinic and a health clinic helping scores of our neighbors here in Oxford Circle with their legal and medical problems.

But we will never suppose that all people need is a better job. They also need Jesus. They need the risen Jesus to forgive their sins, live in their hearts, and give them the power to say no to destructive lifestyles.

So all through our social programs of tutoring and job training, etc. we will gently, sensitively share Jesus. All our staff will be praying for the right opportunity to tell people in our programs that Jesus loves them and wants to become their Lord and Savior. I dream that hundreds and hundreds of people will come to faith in Christ. And I dream that as Christ begins to transform them, we, as Christ's body, will throw our arms around them, walking with them, helping them to wholeness.

I imagine that twenty years from now, blocks and blocks of Oxford Circle around our church and community center are being transformed. Housing, education, family life, and family incomes are all improved. Racial and ethnic reconciliation is demonstrated every day on our streets. Philadelphia politicians know that a whole section of Oxford Circle is a better place. They also know that it is happening because there are Christians at this church as well as many other churches that love Jesus with all their heart; Christians who know that Jesus loves the whole person; Christians who know that people need Jesus and a job.

My sisters and brothers, I don't know how much of that vision will happen in the next twenty years. But I know that with Jesus, all things are possible. I know that what I imagine for Oxford Circle Christian Community Development Association has already happened in many other ministries across the US that are working on John Perkins's model . And that model of course is really just Jesus' vision given to us in his teaching on the gospel of the kingdom.

So let's put our hands in the hands of Jesus. Let's believe that he wants to do great things through Oxford Circle Mennonite Church. Today we are just a little body of believers, but I believe Jesus wants us to grow and expand into a much larger congregation of committed Christians.

Knowing that people need Jesus and a job, let's love the whole person. As we do, God will use this small body of Christians to bring joy and wholeness to dozens, even hundreds and hundreds of our neighbors.

Chapter 9: The Amish, the Cross, and Violence Today

[A sermon preached on October 22, 2006 in the Princeton University Chapel in Princeton, New Jersey.]

FOR ALMOST A WEEK after October 2, 2006, the story of the murder of the little Amish girls captured the attention of America and indeed the world. All our major newspapers and TV news programs ran prominent stories and pictures of long lines of Amish buggies.

But what most amazed everyone was the response of the Amish community. They publicly extended forgiveness to the murderer of their little girls. They even helped raise funds to care for the family of the vicious killer.

At the end of Channel 12's evening news hour with Jim Lehrer, a commentator offered a lengthy, profound reflection on the Amish response. The commentator obviously stood in awe of the Amish expression of forgiveness.

Why? Because forgiveness is not the normal human response to those who attack us. In fact, interspersed with the commentator's reflection on the Amish response and vivid pictures of Amish buggies were snapshots of terrorists around the world doing vengeance for previous injury.

That is the normal response: an eye for an eye. Violence and vengeance lead to more violence and vengeance in a downward spiral towards chaos, destruction, and death.

I believe the Amish got it right. I believe their communal response of forgiveness sprang from the core of Christian faith.

At the center of the biblical story is the awesome reality of the cross. But the cross of Jesus makes sense only in the context of the whole biblical story. A loving, all-powerful, holy God created free human beings in God's very image. God made them stewards of God's awesomely beautiful, complex creation. And God invited them to respond in worship and obedience. But we rebelled, choosing to make ourselves and our own desires the center of the universe rather than God. And the result has been terrible havoc in our homes, our societies, and our inner selves. We have betrayed, oppressed, and killed our neighbors on a colossal scale.

What was God's response? God is the perfect combination of holiness and mercy. God's blazing holiness means that God cannot tolerate evil when we sin against our neighbor. Precisely because God loves everyone, God's holy wrath blazes intensely against those who harm and destroy others made in God's image. But God's astounding love and mercy means that God will not forsake us even in our rebellion and evil. So God acts to correct evil, injustice, and sin.

Let me tell you about a set of experiences in my own personal life that helped me understand God's astounding combination of holiness and mercy.

My wife, Arbutus, and I have lived together for forty-six years of what Richard Foster rightly calls a mixture of ecstasy and halitosis. Mostly it has been joy.

But there have also been times of struggle. The most painful time came in our late thirties. No, we did not commit adultery. But we caused each other great pain. Sadly I must confess that there were times when my anger at Arbutus blazed so furiously that I wanted to hurt her deeply. Partly to wound her and partly to satisfy sinful desires, I would probably have had an adulterous affair but for one thing.

I knew it was sin. I knew our holy God hated adultery. I knew I could not break my marriage vow and still look freely into the loving eyes of my Lord. God's righteous commands protected me when my strength was weak. The biblical truth about God's holiness guarded my step and kept me from inflicting still more pain on the person I loved more than anyone else in the world.

That is not, however, to pretend that I had not sinned against Arbutus. We had inflicted great pain on each other. Our marriage was in crisis. There were days when I wondered if it would survive.

Precisely in those days, I gained a deeper understanding of the cross. As I pondered the wounds that we had inflicted on each other, I realized we had only three choices.

One possibility was to pretend that our sins against each other were not very important—that they did not really matter very much. But that would have been an absurd lie. It hurt terribly.

Another possibility was to shout in anger: "That's it! I'll never forgive you." But that would have ended our relationship forever.

There was just one other possibility. I had to say to Arbutus and she had to say to me: "Your actions were wrong. They hurt me terribly. But I love you. I love you so much that I will take the evil you have done into my heart and forgive you. I can't say it was nothing. But I don't want to live forever estranged and hostile. So I will accept the wounds of your betrayal and purify them with my love and forgiveness."

My friends, that's what the God of the universe was doing at the cross. Our sins are too awful for our holy God to wink at them. Yet, God's love is too strong for God to abandon us. So God embraces our sin, absorbs the evil we have done into God's divine heart, and accepts the punishment we deserve—all because God wants to walk with us again face to face in openness and reconciliation and holiness.

That is the most amazing solution to the problem of evil the world has ever seen. No other religion dares to teach that the Creator of the universe died for the sins of evil human beings. The cross is the only satisfactory solution to the brokenness, violence, and agony of our world.

The cross, however, only makes sense if we understand the God revealed in the Bible. We must remember that God is righteous sovereign as well as loving father. If anything is clear in the Scriptures, it is that blazing holiness and overflowing mercy are both central to God's nature. Jesus taught us more clearly than anyone before or since that the awesome creator of the galaxies is a tender, loving father who delights in our calling him Papa. But the same Jesus repeatedly warned that sinners will depart eternally from this holy God.

The modern church wants to accept only half of God. It seeks to renegotiate God's revelation. It substitutes a new covenant and a new God who offers forgiveness without holiness.

The modern church wants a cosmic Santa Claus who produces wealth, health, and happiness to bolster our good feelings and self-esteem. We prefer a divine buddy who smiles kindly at sin and says: "Aw, shucks, pal, we all mess up sometimes."

The modern church wants to forget sin. We prefer to write our own guidelines for happiness.

The modern church wants to neglect repentance and sanctification. We prefer to replace holiness with happiness.

The biblical God beckons us to return and rediscover who God really is. God summons us to bow in awe before God's searing holiness as we praise God for God's astounding love. Only then will the church truly understand God, sin, and salvation. Only then will it recover its strength. Christians today will remain weak and ineffective until they embrace the full biblical God of searing holiness and overflowing mercy.

Whenever I think carefully about the cross of Jesus, I find myself utterly amazed.

Jesus, the carpenter from Nazareth, became an amazing kind of wandering teacher. He associated with lepers, prostitutes, despised tax collectors, and poor folks. He healed the sick and fed the hungry. He said the messianic kingdom of peace and justice long predicted by the prophets was breaking into history in his person and work.

He also made astonishing claims. He said he was Lord of the Sabbath, one of the most sacred aspects of first-century Jewish life. He claimed divine authority to forgive sins even though the religious leaders promptly denounced this as blasphemy. At his trial he acknowledged that he was the Son of God.

Jesus also clearly understood that he would die for the sake of others. All four versions of the eucharistic words from the Last

Supper (carefully handed down in the church's oral tradition) say, "This is my blood of the covenant which is poured out for many for the forgiveness of sins" (Matthew 26:28). Jesus' death was the sacrificial inauguration of the new covenant.

Paul explains the meaning of the cross most clearly. All people have sinned against God and neighbor. Our holy God hates sin and therefore we all stand condemned and guilty before our just, holy God. But Jesus, the one who committed no sin, took our sin upon himself and became sin for us. At the cross, Jesus took our place so that we could receive divine forgiveness no matter how awful our evil deeds.

Nothing discloses the horror of sin as fully as the cross. The cross is no cheap declaration of indulgent amnesty. Sin is an outrageous affront to God's holiness. It would be a horrible, intolerable world if sin and injustice could continue to rampage and destroy, forever unpunished. The cross demonstrates that the holy sovereign of the universe will not tolerate that. Sin's penalty must be paid.

But the cross is not the sacrifice of a human victim on the altar of an angry, hostile deity. That would deny the doctrines of the incarnation and the Trinity. Father, Son, and Holy Spirit suffer at the cross. It is the Trinitarian God who bears the penalty of our sin.

That means two utterly astounding things.

First it means that no matter how badly you and I have messed up, no matter how vile or vast our sinful actions, our holy, loving God stands with arms outstretched, eagerly longing to forgive us totally and unconditionally if we will just turn and ask for the forgiveness Jesus accomplished for us on the cross.

What an incredible, liberating truth! God invites everyone of us imperfect human beings to live daily with the joyful assurance that our sins are fully forgiven in Christ.

But that is only half of the meaning of the cross. The cross tells us not only that our holy God forgives us disobedient enemies. The cross also tells us that God wants us to treat our enemies the same way. That is what the Amish were doing in such an amazing way. We are all familiar with Jesus' call in the Sermon on the Mount to love our enemies.

But what is the theological foundation of Jesus' call for costly, nonretaliatory love, even for enemies? Jesus did not say that one should practice loving nonviolence because it would always transform vicious enemies into bosom friends. The cross stands as a harsh reminder that love for enemies does not always work—at least not in the short run. Jesus grounds his call to love enemies, not in the hope of reciprocity, but rather in the very nature of God. "Love your enemies and pray for those who persecute you, that you may be children of your Father in heaven. He causes his sun to rise on the evil and the good, and sends rain on the righteous and unrighteous" (Matthew 5:44–45). Jesus said the same thing in the Beatitudes: "Blessed are the peacemakers for they will be called children of God" (Matthew 5:9). God continues to love us even when we make ourselves enemies of God. Instead of promptly destroying sinners, God continues to shower the good gifts of creation upon us. Since that is the way God acts, those who want to be God's sons and daughters must do likewise.

Jesus' conception of the suffering Messiah who goes to the cross as a ransom for sinners takes us to the very center of our understanding of God's way of dealing with enemies. At the Last Supper, Jesus stated unequivocally that he was going to die for the sake of others. "This is my body which is for you"(1 Corinthians 11:24). "This is my blood of the covenant which is poured out for many for the forgiveness of sins" (Matthew 26:28). It is the one who taught his followers to imitate God's love for enemies who now dies with a forgiving prayer on his lips for the enemies who nailed him to the cross (Luke 23:34).

That the cross is the ultimate demonstration that God deals with God's enemies through suffering love receives its clearest theological expression in Paul. In Romans 5, Paul says: "God demonstrates his own love for us in this. While we were still sinners, Christ died for us. . . . While we were God's enemies, we were reconciled to him through the death of his Son" (Romans 5:8, 10). Jesus' vicarious cross for sinners is the foundation and deepest expression of Jesus' command to love one's enemies. As the substitutionary view of the atonement shows, we are enemies in the double sense that sinful persons are hostile to God and that the just holy Creator hates sin (Romans 1:18). For those who know the law, failure to obey it results in the divine curse. But Christ redeemed us from the curse by becoming a curse for us (Galatians 3:10–14). Jesus' blood on the cross was an expiation (Romans 5:18) for us sinful enemies of God because the one who knew no sin was made sin for us on the cross (2 Corinthians 5:21).

At the cross, God suffered for God's enemies. Certainly we can never fathom all the mystery there. But it is precisely because the one hanging limp on the middle cross was the Word become flesh that we are absolutely sure of two interrelated things. First, that a just, holy God mercifully accepts sinful enemies. And second, that God wants us to go and treat all of our enemies in the same merciful, self-sacrificial way.

I think that this truth is not just for the Amish in their response to an individual killer. I think forgiveness is finally the only way to escape the ghastly cycles of violence in our world. Whether the setting is Northern Ireland, Israel-Palestine, South Africa during apartheid, Chechnya, Sri Lanka, India, Pakistan— the list is almost endless—everywhere we see vicious evil followed by a response of vengeance that provokes more vengeance. The agony never ends.

The only alternative to the brokenness and devastation in our world is forgiveness. I am not talking about a naïve optimism that supposes that people are basically good. I am not talking about a cheap forgiveness that fails to face the full horror of evil.

But I am talking about husbands and wives truly forgiving each other for sinful betrayal after they honestly face and confess the evil done. I am talking about Christian communities forgiving murderers. And I am talking about whole societies choosing to forgive terrible evil.

South Africa and its Truth and Reconciliation Commission led by Archbishop Tutu is a wonderful example. Both sides, but especially white Afrikaners, had destroyed and murdered other people. It would have been totally impossible to have had a decent, reconciled society on the other side of apartheid if the new government had decided to seek out and punish every act of evil under apartheid. Instead, Archbishop Tutu's Truth and Reconciliation Commission had the authority to pardon all who came forward and acknowledged their evil deeds. At a profound level, society in South Africa chose forgiveness over vengeance. South Africa did at a societal level what the Amish did in a small community.

It seems to me that that same approach is the only way to end the terrible cycles of violence that spin on and on around our world.

And it seems to me that Christians, Christians who understand the cross; Christians who know the liberating truth that they now stand forgiven in spite of their sin; Christians who know that God wants us to treat our enemies the way God treated us enemies at the cross; it seems to me that Christians should lead the way in offering forgiveness to their enemies and also in helping societies find new ways to choose forgiveness rather than vengeance.

I conclude with one concrete example of how we might do that today in a new way. We are all familiar with the way Dr. Martin Luther King, Jr. and Mahatma Gandhi called on their followers to love their enemies even as they opposed their injustice. And they won stunning victories! Gandhi conquered the British Empire. Dr. King changed American history. There have been astonishing nonviolent campaigns in Poland and in the Philippines that defied and conquered brutal dictatorships.

This past year, Christian Peacemaker Teams have been in the news as one of their members was martyred in Iraq. Christian Peacemaker Teams are at work in a variety of conflict situations around the world, including Israel-Palestine. They love both sides and plead with all to listen to each other and create a just solution for everyone.

Imagine what would happen if the Christian church would train and launch 10,000 Christian peacemaker teams who would move into the most dangerous, most violent areas of our world, and say: "We come in the name of the God of love who calls us to love even our enemies. We beg you to stop killing each other. We will walk with you as you choose to forgive each other for the atrocities of the past and work out ways to live together in cooperation and justice."

Constantly responding to violence with retaliation, vengefully demanding an eye for an eye, finally does not work. May the witness of the Amish point us all to the crucified and risen Lord. May we seek his divine power not only to rest secure in God's awesome forgiveness but also to offer the same forgiveness to our neighbors, even our enemies

Chapter 10: If Christ Be Lord

[A sermon preached at First Presbyterian Church of Bethlehem, Pennsylvania, on November 12, 1978, and then at least eight times in the next six years in North America, England, and India.]

LOOKING BACK ON JESUS' life on the evening of Passover just after Jesus had been crucified, the disciples must have been perplexed by the carpenter's paradoxical life. After living a normal life for about thirty years, Jesus had become a very unusual itinerant teacher. In spite of the fact that Sabbath observance was one of the most sacred aspects of Jewish religious life of the time, he permitted his disciples to break the rules. And when the religious leaders complained, he claimed to be Lord of the Sabbath. When a paralytic sufferer came to him for healing, he forgave his sins. When the Jewish leaders complained that this was blasphemy for God alone can forgive sins, Jesus replied: "Which is easier to say to this paralyzed man, 'Yours sins are forgiven' or to say 'Get up, take your mat and walk'? But I want you to know that the Son of Man has authority on earth to forgive sins." So Jesus said to the man, "I tell you, get up, take your mat and go home" (Mark 2:9–11). And at his trial before the Sanhedrin (the Jewish high court), when they asked him if he was the Messiah, the Son of God, he declared: "I am; . . . and you will see the Son of Man sitting at the right hand of the Mighty One" (Mark 14:62). One understands why monotheistic Jews condemned him as a blasphemer.

Without question, the most amazing and offensive thing about Christianity is that Christians make such outrageous claims about the person of Jesus. Every religious person around the world will gladly accept Jesus of Nazareth as one of the greatest prophets and moral teachers. But Christians insist on adding that Jesus also claimed to be the Son of God. The carpenter from Nazareth, Christians assert, is the Lord of the Universe! That offends! Because he claimed to be the unique Son of God he could say, "I am the way, and the truth, and the life. No one comes to the Father except through me" (John 14:6). That offends!

The perfectly astounding, outrageous nature of Jesus' claims escapes those of us who have grown up in Christian families in "Christian" countries. No other major world religion claims that its founder was God incarnate. Muslims revere Muhammad but they make it very clear he was only a prophet. Monotheistic Jews are equally careful about how they speak of Moses. It was outrageous and blasphemous for the monotheistic Paul to paraphrase the lofty monotheistic passage of Isaiah 45:23 and insist that at the name of Jesus every knee must bow (cf. Isaiah 45:23 with Philippians 2:9–11). It was outrageous and blasphemous for a carpenter from Nazareth to claim to be the Son of God—unless, of course, he was!

Why do Christians make such unusual claims? In his first sermon after Pentecost, Peter declared that it was the resurrection which confirmed Jesus' claim (Acts 2:32–36). In Romans 1:4, Paul says Jesus was "appointed the Son of God in power by his resurrection from the dead." The resurrection removed the uncertainty and ambiguity about the identity of Jesus and made it clear that the carpenter from Nazareth was Lord of the universe. Jesus is Lord.

The fact that Jesus is Lord has all kinds of implications for us. If Jesus of Nazareth was not just another prophet, but rather God in the flesh, then we must joyfully submit to all his teaching. We cannot pick out those parts of his message that sound agreeable to us, our friends and our subculture and ignore the rest. We cannot accept his command to free the poor and oppressed and ignore his command to make disciples of all nations. We dare not so emphasize the fact that he came to reveal a perfect ethical model that we forget that he also came to die for our sins. We dare not claim to oppose racism and war on his authority and then ignore his call to sexual purity. If he is Lord, then we must joyfully open our lives unconditionally to all his truth and to all his commands.

At the same time, however, submission to Jesus' lordship frees us from all other lords. In fact, there are no other lords who can demand our unconditional, unquestioning obedience. If Jesus is Lord, then the American President is not lord, the Russian ruler is not lord, the Pentagon is not Lord, the president of my college or company is not lord. If Jesus is Lord, then neither success nor prestige nor middle-class values nor left-wing nor right-wing ideology is lord. Accepting Jesus' lordship gives us a radical new freedom. We can respect presidents and human institutions as long as they make just, limited demands, but their power is finally very weak. Only Jesus is absolute Lord.

The fact that Jesus is Lord relates directly to the story of the rich young ruler (Luke 18:18–25). The funny thing about Jesus is that when he talked to the rich young ruler, he seemed more concerned about costly discipleship than about getting a prosperous supporter to join his movement. In fact, Jesus seems to have gone out of his way to warn people about the cost of becoming his disciples. He made it crystal clear that it had to be all or nothing.

Jesus did not try to make becoming his follower as easy as possible. He was not interested in church growth at the expense of faithful discipleship.

When his popularity spread and large crowds swarmed around him, he stated the demands of discipleship harshly: "If anyone comes to me and does not hate father and mother, wife and children, brothers and sisters—yes, even life itself—such a person cannot be my disciple . . . Those of you who do not give up everything you have cannot be my disciples" (Luke 14:25–33).

It's all or nothing. Jesus and his kingdom must be the pearl of great price for which we are ready unconditionally to abandon absolutely everything else in our lives if necessary—or we cannot be Jesus' disciple at all.

Notice what Jesus did not say to the rich young man who came to him. Jesus did not tell him: "Just say a short prayer and I'll forgive you and give you inner peace, a happy family life, and success in business." Jesus spelled out the demands of discipleship as sharply as possible. If you want to be my disciple, Jesus said, then I must be total, absolute Lord of your life. You will have to sell all your goods because money is your idol.

Jesus says the same things to us today. To those of us who want to be his disciples, he insists that that means he must become absolute Lord of our personal family budgets, Lord of our business practices, and Lord of our involvement in the economic structures of our affluent society. Jesus won't be a supernatural psychoanalyst who brings inner psychological peace, marital bliss, and happy families and then politely declines to ask how our economic lifestyle relates to starvation in inner-city Chicago and rural South America. "Those of you who do not give up everything you have cannot be my disciples."

Now all this makes me fear and tremble. I have the same feelings of uneasiness you do. Sometimes I wish the God of the poor were less concerned about how I earn and spend my money. But God is—so you and I must choose.

Either we surrender our total selves to Jesus as unconditional Lord and Master or we cannot be his disciples—at least that's what he said. And when we do say yes to him as Lord, he accepts us just as we are and begins to remake us according to the model of his own self-giving love.

If Christ is to be our total Lord today, then there are two key things that are important:

1. First, we need to understand the world we live in so that our lives in this world are shaped by his teaching and his plans rather than our sinful neighbors.

2. Second, we need to understand the biblical teaching on structural evil or systemic sin.

First, our world today. Not only are we rich and others poor. Our affluence depends to some degree on their poverty. There is not time here to cite the evidence for that statement, but I have written about that in my book, *Rich Christians in an Age of Hunger.*

Our world is militaristic, our world is sexually perverted, our world is tragically and dangerously divided between rich and poor. But it is precisely here in this good but fallen creation that the Risen Prince of Peace wants us to follow him as absolute Lord.

If we are to do that in a biblically faithful way, then we need to understand not just our world, but also the biblical teaching on structural injustice, or structural sin.

There is an important difference between consciously willed individual acts like, say, lying to a friend or committing an act of adultery, and participation in evil social structures. Slavery was an example of an institutionalized evil. So was the Victorian factory system where ten-year-old children worked twelve to sixteen hours a day. Both were legal, but they destroyed millions of people. They were institutionalized or structural evils.

In the twentieth century, although not in the eighteenth or nineteenth, some Christians, especially evangelical Christians, have been mostly concerned with personal sins. But the Bible cares about both. Speaking through the prophet Amos, the Lord declares, "For three sins of Israel, even for four, I will not turn back my wrath" (i.e., revoke the punishment). Why? Because "they sell the innocent for silver, and the needy for a pair of sandals. They trample on the heads of the poor as on the dust of the ground, and deny justice to the oppressed." Thus far, the text is talking about oppression of the poor. But the text goes on to say God will also punish Israel because "father and son use the same girl and so profane my holy name" (Amos 2:6–7).

Biblical scholars have shown that some kind of legal fiction underlies the phrase "selling the needy for a pair of sandals." This mistreatment of the poor was legal. In one breath, notice too, God condemns both sexual misconduct and legalized oppression of the poor. Sexual sins and economic injustice are equally displeasing to the God of Scripture.

One of the tragedies of our own time is that some young activists have supposed that as long as they were fighting for the rights of minorities and opposing militarism, they were morally righteous regardless of how often they shacked up for the night with a guy or a girl in the movement. And some of their parents, on the other hand, supposed that because they didn't steal, lie, and fornicate, they were morally upright even though they lived in segregated communities and owned stock in companies that oppressed the poor of the earth. But Scripture says that both of those things are equally serious to God. Robbing one's workers of a fair wage is just as sinful as robbing a bank.

God also shows that laws themselves are sometimes an abomination to God. Psalm 94:20 condemns a corrupt ruler who "brings on misery by [his] decrees." The Jerusalem Bible has an excellent rendition of verse 20. It says: "You never consent [that is, you should never consent] to that corrupt tribunal that imposes disorder as law." God wants God's people to know that wicked governments sometimes frame mischief by statute. Or as the New English Bible puts it: "They contrive evil under cover of law." God proclaims the same word through the prophet Isaiah: "Woe to those who make unjust laws, to those who issue oppressive decrees." Why do they do that? The text tells us: "To deprive the poor of their rights and withhold justice from the oppressed of my people" (Isaiah 10:1–2). It is quite possible to work oppression legally. But legalized oppression is an abomination to God, and therefore God commands God's people to oppose it.

There is one other side to social or institutionalized evil that makes it especially pernicious. Social evil is so subtle that one can be caught up in it without realizing it. God inspired the prophet Amos to utter some of the harshest words in Scripture against the cultured, upper-class women of the day. "Hear this word, you cows of Bashan . . ." That is not nice, polite language. But the prophet goes on to say why he speaks so harshly about the women: "You women who oppress the poor and crush the needy, and say to your husbands, 'Bring us some drinks!' The Sovereign Lord has sworn by his holiness: the time will surely come when you will be taken away with hooks, the last of you with fishhooks" (Amos 4:1–2).

Now the women involved probably had no contact or very little contact with the impoverished peasants. They may never have realized clearly that their gorgeous clothes and spirited parties were possible only because of the sweat and tears of toiling peasants. In fact, they may even have been kind to individual peasants that they met. Perhaps they gave them "Christmas baskets" once a year. But God called these privileged ladies "cows" because they profited from social evil. Hence they were personally and individually guilty before God.

It seems to me that that means that if one is a member of a privileged class that profits from social evil, and if one at least partially understands that connection and does nothing to try to change it, then one stands guilty before God. Social evil or structural evil is just as sinful as personal sin. And it's a lot more subtle.

What does this biblical teaching on structural evil mean for us as Christians, as ministers, as lawyers, doctors, homemakers, union members, businesspeople, and teachers? It means that the risen Jesus wants to be Lord of our every decision in our area of daily work. It means that Jesus' teaching and biblical values should be just as important and decisive for us in the corporate board room as in our personal sexual practices.

There are a lot of wonderful Christians who are also lawyers, doctors, and businesspeople. But there are far fewer Christian lawyers, Christian doctors, and Christian businesspeople. There are many Christians in the professions who try to use their professional contacts to witness to others about Christ. And that is excellent. We need more of that. But that is not enough. If Christ is to be Lord of our life as teachers and businesspeople, if we are to be Christian lawyers, not just lawyers who are also believers, then we must allow every area of our life as teachers, lawyers, and businesspeople to be shaped and informed by biblical standards.

That will mean bringing central biblical doctrines like God's special concern for the poor and God's demand for justice for the oppressed into our business decisions. That will mean insisting that justice for the poor is more important than profits regardless of what the stockholders say. That will mean asking how just the total company we work for is, or how just the present structures of our profession are. That will mean becoming a loving critic of the legal profession or the health profession for the sake of God's poor.

Obviously that is not an easy task. It is far easier to restrict Christ—as most professional people who are Christians have done—to the area of personal moral issues like lying and stealing and sexual morality. But Christ will not be half a Lord. He calls us to accept him as total Lord—and that means he wants us as professional people to strive to make the area of society where we work more just according to biblical standards .

The biblical call to put justice and the needs of the poor above profits and job security raises the question of Jesus' Lordship in a sharp, personal way. Obviously, that will cost us something. We will undoubtedly have to choose, perhaps frequently, between professional promotion and persisting in our demand for business practices that are more just, between social status and persistent championing of the rights of minorities. And in each case, we will also be choosing between Mammon and Jesus. In each case we will be telling our children and the world whether our Christian faith is a social convenience or a total, unconditional commitment to Jesus as absolute Lord.

I believe there are millions and millions of Christians in this country who want to do that regardless of the cost. Millions and millions of Christians who would rather have Jesus than houses or lands. They know with St. Matthew that all authority in heaven and earth has been given to the risen Lord Jesus.

I dream of thousands and thousands of Christian lawyers who will apply biblical standards of justice to the legal profession. I dream of thousands and thousands of Christian businesspeople who will make God's special concern for the poor central in corporate board rooms. I dream of thousands and thousands of Christian nurses and doctors who will transform our hospitals and health delivery system so the poor are cared for as well as the rich. I dream of millions of biblical Christians who will, by God's grace, submit every area of their life to Christ as Lord.

Will you and I dare to join them? In our own strength, that is impossible, but not with God. For all things are possible with God. Amen.

PART THREE: Baptism, Ordination, and Holy Communion

Chapter 11: **Baptized Into Life**

[A sermon preached on the occasion of the baptism of my son, Michael Jay Sider, on January 9, 1983 at Diamond St. Mennonite Church in Philadelphia.]

BAPTISM IS THE GATEWAY to life—to genuine life, to full, joyous life, to the richest, most fulfilling life there is. At baptism, we are baptized into life.

Now, just a minute, someone will say. Do you mean that the water of baptism has some mysterious power that automatically guarantees a wonderful life? Of course not. There is nothing magical about water baptism. What matters is accepting the gospel, not baptism (1 Corinthians 1:16–17). But baptism is a sign that you have accepted the gospel. Baptism is a public confession that you believe in your heart that Jesus died for your sins and that you have invited Christ to be King and Master of your life. Baptism is a public confession that you have entered into a living personal relationship with the Author of Life. Baptism is your public announcement to anybody who is listening—whether family, church, world, or the devil himself—that you are betting your life on the One who promises to give abundant life. Baptism is the gateway to life—to gutsy, wildly exciting, costly, meaning-packed living.

At least, that's what St. Paul seems to think. Paul has a clear answer to the important question: How do you really find genuine life? Paul says there are just two possibilities: life or death. We have to choose one or the other. And he says that Jesus is the way to life and sin is the way to death. We must choose between life and death, between Christ and sin.

Now I know it seldom seems that simple. It seldom seems that clear-cut. There are all kinds of views around today about how to live a joyous, happy life. There are all kinds of things that promise to offer a swinging, frolicking, fulfilled life. And you can be sure that they don't advertise themselves by the names or labels of sin and death.

Power, fame, sex, money, self-centeredness all claim to offer the way to life. I'd be a liar if I said their promises were not appealing.

Money says: Join me, friend. Wealth is the way to real living. Money means everything you want—expensive clothes, a lovely house, exotic Hawaiian vacations, backpacking in the Swiss Alps and the Asian Himalayans. Man, that's living!

Modern sexual thinking says the way to life is sexual liberation. All that old-fashioned stuff about waiting till marriage to enjoy the ecstasy of sex and then the even sillier notion of restricting yourself to your wife or husband—man, that's not just old-fashioned, that's a sure route to a slow, boring death. The modern way is to be cool, to sleep around, to sample the exciting variety of many partners before and after marriage. Wow! That's living. That's the way to a thrilling life!

The self, the ego, has its own tempting offer for each of us. There aren't any absolute standards, the ego says. Each person is his own king. Whatever feels good to you is true and good for you. Aim to please yourself. Use other people for your own goals and ambitions. Don't trample on other people unnecessarily because that makes unnecessary enemies and is counter-productive. But get ahead, make a career for yourself, even if it does mean ignoring, hurting, or crawling over other people. You are the center of the universe. Sophisticated, subtle, calculating self-centeredness—that's the way to a fulfilling life.

Who is right? St. Paul or money, sex, or self? All of us have to answer that question every week of our lives. But the questions are more pressing at certain periods of our lives. At no time are these questions more urgent, more difficult, than in the teenage years.

It often amazes me, in fact, it frightens me, to realize that in the few short years between thirteen and twenty, young people have to make almost all the important decisions of life. You have to decide who you are. You have to decide what your basic goals and values are in life. You have to decide where and what to study. You have to decide what career you want to have. You have to decide your attitudes toward money and power, sex and fame. You have to consider picking a marriage partner knowing that that other person will be the source of the most joy or the most hell for all the rest of your life.

If you look carefully, you will discover that at the core, at the center, of each of these different, difficult decisions is the same basic question: What is the way to genuine life? What is the gateway to rich, abundant living?

Let's look more closely at St. Paul's answer. Paul says that it is quite possible to choose these other things—money, power, sex, self-centeredness. But if we do, they grab us and enslave us. We become slaves to them. The only alternative is to choose Christ; to surrender ourselves to him. Listen to the way Paul puts it in Romans 6:16–22:

> Don't you know that when you offer yourselves to someone as obedient slaves, you are slaves of the one you obey— whether you are slaves to sin, which leads to death, or to obedience, which leads to righteousness? But thanks be to God that though you used to be slaves to sin, you have come to obey from your heart the pattern of teaching that has now claimed your allegiance. You have been set free from sin and have become slaves to righteousness. I am using an example from everyday life because of your human limitations. Just as you used to offer yourselves as slaves to impurity and to ever-increasing wickedness, so now offer yourselves as slaves to righteousness leading to holiness. When you were slaves to sin, you were free from the control of righteousness. What benefit did you reap at that time from the things you are now ashamed of? Those things result in death! But now that you have been set free from sin and have become slaves of God, the benefit you reap

leads to holiness, and the result is eternal life. For the
wages of sin is death, but the gift of God is eternal life in
Christ Jesus our Lord.

True freedom comes only in Christ. Genuine life comes
only in surrendering our lives to Christ. Now that does not mean
that we never experience money or sex or power or self-fulfillment. God after all is the creator of all those things. God knows
how they are supposed to be used and enjoyed. When we start
by surrendering those things to Christ, we then learn how he as
the Creator intends us to enjoy money, sex, power, and our own
egos. When we say no to all those things for the sake of Christ,
we get all those things back again. As Jesus said: "Seek ye first the
Kingdom of God and his righteousness and all these things shall
be added unto you." That doesn't mean we will have all those
things in exactly the way our small, sinful minds think we would
like them. But it does mean that we will have those things in the
ways that will be good for us.

You know, some people do it backwards and then everything
gets messed up. I know people who made their decisions about
their wife or husband and their career while in rebellion against
God. Later on, they wanted to come back to Christ. But then everything was doubly difficult. Their spouse was not a Christian
and had little sympathy for Christian faith. Other sinful choices
also made it much harder to choose Christ.

It is absolutely crucial that you young people settle the big
question first. Make your biggest decision, your decision about
Jesus, before you make the other weighty decisions about spouse,
job, and lifestyle. Choose Christ first. Choose life in Christ. Walk
through the only genuine gateway to life and then the other decisions will be easier. They'll still be tough and difficult, but they will
be easier because your foundation will be solid.

That's why it is so exciting that two of the persons to be baptized today are young people. They are settling the big question
first. Thank God we can come to Christ later in life. Thank God
we can enter the gateway to abundant life when we are forty or
fifty or sixty or seventy. But thank God for the privilege of walking

through the gateway to life while still young, while almost all of your life still lies before you .

We have looked at the fact that Paul says that Jesus is the way to life. Now I want to examine his teaching a little more closely because there are three important paradoxes in this text from Paul.

You know what I mean by a paradox. A paradox is something that is different from what it seems to be. In a paradox we have two things joined together that don't seem to fit together. The Trinity is a paradox. God is one and yet the one God consists of three persons. Or we might speak of a happy sorrow at the death of a beloved Christian mother who had suffered severely before passing on to be with Christ.

Well, there are three paradoxes in Paul's teaching about Christ as the gateway to life:

1. First, Paul says that death (in a figurative sense) is the way to life.

2. Second, Paul says that in the Christian life God does it all and yet we still do it too.

3. Third, Paul says that even death in the literal sense is the way to life.

Let's look at each of these paradoxes.

How is death the way to life? Paul says that at baptism, believers are baptized into death! The title of this sermon is "Baptized Into Life" and I have been claiming that Christ is the way to life. But in our text, Paul says that at baptism we die and are buried. What is the apostle talking about?

Listen to Romans 6:3–8:

> Don't you know that all of us who were baptized into Christ Jesus were baptized into his death? We were therefore buried with him through baptism into death in order that, just as Christ was raised from the dead through the glory of the father, we too may live a new life. If we have been united with him in a death like his, we will certainly also be united with him in a resurrection like his. For we know that our old self was crucified with him so that

the body ruled by sin might be done away with, that we
should no longer be slaves to sin—because anyone who
has died has been set free from sin. Now if we died with
Christ, we believe that we will also live with him.

It will help us to understand this passage if we remember
that baptism by immersion was the common practice of the early
church. The form is not very important but when Paul was present
at a baptism, the person's whole body would be completely immersed under the water. Paul says that gives us a clue about what
baptism and personal conversion truly mean.

Every person is self-centered at birth. As we get older, this
basic selfishness expresses itself in all kinds of sin. We have talked
about the way this selfishness can take the form of worshipping
sex or power or money. In order to choose Christ, we must say no
to all these idols and place Christ at the center of our lives. When
we do that, we actually die to our old self. We bury, or rather, God
buries, our old selves. In a figurative or spiritual sense, our old
selfish personalities focused on personal ambition, pride in our
good looks or grades or abilities—our old self-centered personalities—have to die.

That's exactly what happens in baptism. Being immersed under the water in baptism is a symbol, a little picture, of the way our
old selves die and are buried with Christ.

But we don't stay dead any more than Jesus remained forever
in the tomb.

Just as Jesus rose from the dead, so too we rise from conversion and baptism into a new life, into a new life in Christ. This is
the very heart of the mystery of Christian faith.

Somehow in a way we will never fully understand, believers
are mystically joined to Christ. Christ comes to live in us. St. Paul
says in Galatians 2:20: "I no longer live but Christ lives in me."
When we enter into a personal, living relationship with Christ,
it is the Risen Sovereign of this whole universe that now lives in
you and me. The mighty power of the resurrected Lord Jesus now
flows through us. As we rise from the waters of baptism, we leave
behind our old sinful selves and rise to a new life in the image of

Jesus Christ. But that can happen only if we say no to our old sinful selfish personalities. Death is the way to life.

Rising to a new life in Christ is a fantastic thing because it means that we don't face our struggles, our temptations, our tough decisions about life alone. You young people do have to make all those momentous decisions about career and marriage—but you don't have to do that alone. The mighty power of the Author of life is present in even the most terrifying moments. When the devil roars into your life with his most subtle, most overpowering appeal to choose sexual license or to give in to what the majority is doing even though you know it is wrong, even at that desperate moment when you feel overwhelmed by temptation, the risen Lord is present. He will help you choose life because you have been baptized into Christ, because you have entered the gateway of life.

And the same is true for all of us, no matter what our age, no matter how long we have been Christians. At the toughest moments when the devil seemed overpowering, Martin Luther used to remind Satan that he was a baptized Christian. With Luther, we can tell Satan to go to hell because we have already died to sin in baptism.

We have already been raised to a new life in Christ.

Our first paradox then is that death, i.e., figurative death to our sinful selves, is the only way to life.

But there is a second paradox here. Paul seems to say both that God does it all and also that we have to do it. Have you noticed the extremely strong language Paul uses about God's activity here? He says we have actually died to our old selfish ideas and plans. Our old self has been crucified. He says God has raised us to a new life. It is perfectly clear that this is not something we do. Notice that the verbs are all passive verbs. He does not say we crucify ourselves or raise ourselves. He says we are crucified; we are raised to a new life.

By whom? By God, of course! We could never overcome the powerful selfishness and temptation in our lives by ourselves. But God has already done it. Listen how strongly Paul puts it in verses 6 and 7: "We know that our old self was crucified with him so that the body ruled by sin might be done away with, that we should no longer be slaves to sin—because anyone who has died has been set free from sin."

That sounds like God has already done the whole thing! But when I look carefully at myself, I see that I'm still a stinking sinner in a lot of tragic ways. Sin is still present. And Paul knows that. Right after all these powerful words about how God has buried our old sinful selves and raised up a new self, Paul turns right around and says: Be careful not to sin. Obey God. It's up to you to live the Christian life. Listen to verses 12–13: "Therefore, do not let sin reign in your mortal body so that you obey its evil desires. Do not offer any part of yourself to sin as an instrument of wickedness, but rather offer yourselves to God as those who have been brought from death to life; and offer every part of yourself to him as an instrument of righteousness."

We have a paradox here. Paul says that God has already changed us. God has already done what needs to happen so we can live Christlike lives. But Paul also says the responsibility is ours to live an obedient Christian life.

You see, there are two dangers in the Christian life. Sometimes we think God has done everything and there is nothing left for us to do. Then we get lazy and don't do our best. But the other danger is just as serious. It is a dreadful mistake to think that we are all alone and everything depends on our hard work. Not for a moment. The mighty Author of life is at work in each of us. When temptation seems overpowering, we can rely on God's strength. On the other hand, when we become lazy and careless in the Christian life, we must remember Paul's command to do our very best.

That is our second paradox: Paul tells us that God has already crucified our old sinful selves in Christ, but then he turns around and tells us we had better work hard to say no to the sin that still remains in our lives.

There is one final paradox: death—and now I mean literal death, not figurative dying to sin. Death is the way to life. Paul says we are baptized into Christ's death. That means that the new life we live is the same kind of life Jesus lived. And you know what happened to Jesus. They nailed him to a piece of wood and killed him. And they did it because of the way he lived and what he taught. He cared about the poor and he opposed war and violence.

If you and I are truly baptized into Christ's cross, then we will take the way of the cross today. And that may be dangerous. Thousands and thousands of Christians have become martyrs in the last fifty years because they dared to live the way Jesus lived.

Jim Elliot and others died as missionaries trying to take the gospel to the Auca Indians who had never heard the Good News. Dr. Martin Luther King, Jr. died because he opposed racism. The Catholic sisters in El Salvador died because they sought justice for the poor and oppressed.

To be honest, I have to say to my son, Michael, to all of you who are being baptized, indeed to all of us: Jesus calls you and me to a dangerous, risky adventure. He calls you and me to be ready to lay down our lives for the sake of others—to oppose racism, to seek justice, to share the gospel, to say no to violence.

The ghastly shadow of devastating war hovers over our world. When Jesus opposed war and violence, he got killed. The same may happen today to those who say no to violence. Being baptized into Christ means being ready to die for him.

But even then, death is not the end. Because even physical death is the way to life. Paul promises in verse 5 that "if we have been united with him in a death like his, we will certainly also be united with him in a resurrection like his." If we die opposing racism or war for the sake of Jesus, we will go on to live forever with the risen Lord. For the Christian, death, physical death, is the gateway to eternal life.

You who are to be baptized today walk through a very significant gateway. I promise you struggle, conflict, and difficulty, maybe even death itself. But I also promise you life—adventure packed, joyously fulfilling life now. And life forever in the presence of the Author of life. In the name of the risen Lord, be baptized into his life.

As these brothers and sisters are baptized, I hope all of us will reflect again on the meaning of baptism. As believers, let's renew our baptismal vows. As the water flows over them, may the Holy Spirit flood anew over each of us, putting to death that sin that still troubles us and raising us to new, victorious living in Christ.

If there are any here who have not yet said a solid, unconditional "yes" to Christ, I invite you to make that decision now. Now is the day of salvation. It is so easy to say yes to Christ. Right now in the quiet of your heart you can say to God: "From this moment forward, my God, I choose life in Christ."

Behold, I call heaven and earth to witness this day that I have set before you life and death; therefore choose life.

Chapter 12: **Ordained for Daring Biblical Leadership**

[Given for two of my students: a short ordination charge for Jim Fox on June 15, 1981; and a longer ordination sermon for Darryl Brubaker on June 26, 1988 in Albuquerque, New Mexico.]

MY YOUNG FRIEND, YOU are being ordained to Christian ministry at one of the most dangerous periods in the history of the world. The next few decades will be some of the most perilous that humanity has ever faced.

You take this new step of service of the Prince of Peace at a moment in history when the man in charge of nuclear weapons testing at Los Alamos national laboratory recently told me personally that unless there is major change, the likelihood of nuclear war in the next ten to twenty years is almost 100 percent. You take this new step of service of the defender of the poor at a moment when the growing gap between rich and poor produces dangerous conflict and condemns millions to death by malnutrition. You take this new step of service of the one who celebrated and commanded lifelong covenant in marriage at a time when cultural changes and relativistic values threaten marriage and the family as never before. You take this new step of service of the resurrected one, the surest foundation of hope, at a moment in history when our contemporaries slip deeper and deeper into fatalistic despair. And you take this new step of service of the one who came to die for the sins of the world at a moment in history when there are more and more people every year who have never heard, or now reject, the Good News of Jesus Christ.

Never has there been a more urgent need for holistic biblical faith. Nothing is adequate to the terrifying problems of our time except the whole Bible for the whole person. A one-sided Christian faith that offers personal salvation but neglects justice, freedom, and peace in society or an equally one-sided Christian faith that works to end injustice without proclaiming the glorious forgiveness offered in the cross of God become flesh is simply inadequate for the needs of our time.

People need and want a vibrant, living, personal relationship with Jesus Christ. May the Holy Spirit inspire and guide you to lead many to personal faith in the risen Lord and to train many others to do the same.

Down deep, people also want peace and justice. None of us want to drift blindly toward nuclear holocaust and a scarred earth where a few of our surviving grandchildren wander hopelessly amid the broken ruins of a civilization that has committed suicide. All of us want an end to starvation, an end to broken families, and an end to sexual chaos and marital tragedy.

But our people do not see clearly how to move from the current chaos to the desired goals of peace and justice and wholeness. Often we do not even clearly understand that our present actions and society's present direction lead almost inevitably to tragedy and disaster.

And even when we do substantially understand the problems, we often fail to act, immobilized or seduced by the demand for instant gratification. Demanding instant joy, we abandon our spouse as soon as problems surface. Demanding instant affluence, we tolerate a colossal national debt that will cripple our grandchildren. Demanding instant convenience, we abort unwelcome, inconvenient babies.

You and I are placed as watchmen to God's people today in this confused, broken world in precisely the way the prophets of the Old Testament were sent as watchmen to Israel. Take to heart the words of the prophet Ezekiel (33:1-6):

> Son of man, speak to your people and say to them:
> "When I bring the sword against a land, and the people

of the land choose one of their men and make him their watchman, and he sees the sword coming against the land and blows the trumpet to warn the people, then if anyone hears the trumpet but does not heed the warning and the sword comes and takes their life, their blood will be on their own head. . . . But if the watchman sees the sword coming and does not blow the trumpet to warn the people and the sword comes and takes someone's life, that person's life will be taken because of their sin, but I will hold the watchman accountable for their blood."

God says the same thing to us in our time. God says to us all: Turn to me that you may live. Repent of your foolish ways. Return to my ways of peace, justice, and personal conversion through the blessed presence of the Holy Spirit and you shall live. Return to me and join my people in my redeemed body and you shall live.

My young friend, you are called as a watchman to warn all God's children of impending danger and to share the Good News of hope in Christ. Sometimes it will be hard. Sometimes it will be scary. Sometimes it will be costly.

There is only one way to do it and that is with biblical balance in the power of the Holy Spirit. Preach the whole biblical word. Be a loving nurturing pastor. Together with your wife, model a better way of living in this messed-up world of broken families. Be an evangelist. And also be a prophet.

People can hear even the most threatening message when it comes from someone who has gently and lovingly pastored them. People can hear even the most probing, painful word when they know that you have cried and wept before the Lord in prayer before speaking. People can hear the most vigorous challenge when they know that you submit all you do and say to the standard of God's word.

So be a faithful Christian leader of God's flock.

I want to focus four things that are essential for faithful Christian leadership today.

First, model integrity in your personal life. Paul tells Timothy in 1 Timothy 3:2 to be above reproach. Your relationship with your wife should be a model of integrity. Your child–parent relationships should provide a good example. Your tax forms should illustrate honesty. Constant integrity even in the small things is crucial. We are all constantly tempted, but by God's grace we can resist temptation.

Second, accept your finitude. Our basic sin is to want to be God and refuse to accept our finitude and creaturehood. Our foolish striving for more and more is rooted in this basic sin. We want more and more money, more and more fame. Satan whispers: Would it not be nice if your spouse was a little more beautiful, or a little more sensitive, or a little more intelligent or whatever?

There is always someone else who has more money or more physical beauty or greater speaking ability. Finally that insatiable desire for more and more comes from the basic sin of wanting to be God rather than a finite creature.

Leaders must accept their finitude. It is okay to be just who you are with your strengths and your limitations. Paul does not explicitly tell Timothy to accept his finitude. But you do that when you avoid being a lover of money. You do that when you avoid being puffed up with conceit.

Just being who you are is wonderful! Accept your limitations. Certainly, use all your gifts. Develop your God-given abilities to the full. Be all God wants you to be. But accept your limitations and rejoice in your finitude.

Three, be sure you have a strong structure of accountability. Today there is a rampant individualism among Christian leaders. There is very little accountability. Be sure you have a few people (starting with your wife) who are close to you. People who know beyond any shadow of a doubt that you want them to be ruthlessly honest with you. People who know you want them to challenge you. People who know you want them to say you are wrong or in danger of sinning when they see that.

Stay close to that accountability group. Precisely when you need them the most, you will be tempted to withdraw, to keep something to yourself, to hide the things you most need to share with them.

Four, have the courage to cling to God's word no matter what the cost.

We don't need more so-called Christian leaders who simply repeat what people want to hear. We don't need more Christian leaders who fail to speak God's full word because the congregation or the larger society or the bishop would be offended. Have the guts to say what the Bible and the situation demand to be said.

Cling to God's revealed word. Dare to continue speaking it no matter how unpopular. Have the courage to defy entrenched interests when God's word demands it.

In Amos 7:10–17, the prophet provides a wonderful model. The prophet infuriates the king and the king's priest by announcing that the nation of Israel will go into exile for its sins. The king's priest first tells the king that Amos is committing treason. Then the priest orders Amos to stop preaching his frightening message and go home. In response, Amos insists that God called him to speak this message. Then Amos repeats God's word in even stronger terms!

Dare to announce God's word. All of it! Do that regardless of the response of the congregation.

I've mentioned four things that are crucial for a Christian leader today. First, model integrity in your personal life. Second, accept your finitude. Third, establish a strong structure of accountability. Finally, have the courage to speak the full biblical word.

That sounds impossible. And it is in your own strength. But you don't stand alone. The one who walked among us, died for our sins, was raised from the dead, and now sits at the right hand of the Father, that one actually intercedes for you. Nothing in all creation can tear you from his loving arms.

So take courage. You can be a faithful Christian leader even in these tough times. The Lord is risen indeed. God's final word is not despair, sin, or death. God's final word is resurrection. Go forth as a faithful minister at this dangerous moment in history and preach the glorious news that Jesus still reigns, that Jesus still forgives sinners, that Jesus still empowers his people to work for justice and peace.

We know that the final victory is his. In God's good time, the kingdoms of this world will assuredly become the kingdom of our God and of his Christ. Until that time comes or God calls you home, go forth in the power of the Holy Spirit to preach and live the whole gospel for the whole person for the whole world.

Chapter 13: **The Meaning of Holy Communion**

[A sermon preached on March 30, 2014 at my home congregation, Oxford Circle Mennonite Church in Philadelphia.]

SOMETIMES RITUALS BECOME SO commonplace that we forget or overlook their deep meaning. That can even happen with something so profoundly important as the Lord's Supper. So, since this Sunday is a Sunday when we at Oxford Circle Mennonite Church share in the Lord's Supper, I decided to use my sermon to talk about the meaning of Holy Communion.

Christians have used a variety of terms: the Lord's Supper, Holy Communion, the sacrament of the Eucharist. But these are all different terms for the same ritual—although as you know, Christians over the centuries have understood the practice in different ways.

Like every good sermon, I have three points. To understand Holy Communion, we need to think about three things:

I. The Lord's Cross

II. The Lord's time frame

III. The Lord's body

I. The Lord's Cross

It is almost impossible for us today to really grasp how awful the cross—or the idea of Jesus dying on the cross—was in Jesus' day. We wear crosses around our necks and use the word as an easy symbol of small troubles ("my mother-in-law is a cross I have to bear").

But in Jesus' day the cross was a terrible, ghastly reality. The brutal Roman imperialists crucified thousands—including slaves who rebelled and Jewish Messianic pretenders. They nailed the victims' hands and legs to a wooden cross and left them to hang in agony until they died.

And it wasn't just the awful pain. The Jews knew that the Old Testament said, "Cursed be anyone who hangs on a tree." The Jews also knew that anybody who claimed to be Messiah and then got crucified was a fake, a false pretender. As for the Romans, crucifixion was a symbol of power. It was the cruel way the Romans crushed every threat to their rule.

So for early Christians to say their leader had been crucified was to make an utterly amazing statement. But Paul says in 1 Corinthians 2:2, "I resolved to know nothing while I was with you except Jesus Christ and him crucified." The cross is at the very center of Christian faith.

That is not to say that the cross is the only important part of Christian faith. The resurrection is equally important.

Nor is it to say that the only reason Jesus came was to die. Some Christians make a terrible mistake and reduce the Christian faith to the substitutionary atonement. They reduce Christian faith to Christ taking our sins upon himself at the cross so that we can be forgiven and go to heaven when we die. That is part of salvation, but only one part. To reduce Christian faith just to that is a terrible—heretical—mistake.

Jesus also came to show us how to live—to model a perfect life, to teach us how to love our neighbors—even our enemies. Jesus also came to conquer Satan and death itself by rising from the dead. So the cross is only one part of Christian faith.

But it is a big part. We can see that in two special practices ("sacraments" we now call them)—two special practices of the earliest Christians: baptism and the Lord's Supper.

In Romans 6:3–5, Paul says that in baptism we are "baptized into Christ's death." In baptism, in some profound sense, we are joined with Christ in his death on the cross.

And in the Lord's Supper, as we saw in the text Theresa read, we "proclaim the Lord's death." The bread stands for Jesus' physical body torn and crucified for us. The cup stands for Jesus' blood that ran from his crucified body.

So the cross is absolutely central for Christian faith. But why? What happened at the cross to make it so important?

Paul teaches us in the first three chapters of Romans that all have sinned and deserve God's punishment. All through the Old Testament, the Bible tells us that God is a holy God who hates and punishes sin. But the fantastic Good News of Christianity is that Jesus took our deserved punishment on himself at the cross. That means that you and I are forgiven though the cross. Paul says in 2 Corinthians 5:18–20 that Jesus Christ knew no sin, but he became sin for us. And in Galatians 3:13–14, Paul says Christ redeemed us by becoming a curse for us on the cross. And in Ephesians 1:7, Paul says you and I "have redemption through his blood, the forgiveness of sins."

That means that because of the cross, sinners like you and me—we people who have messed up our lives and hurt our spouses, children, families, and neighbors—sinners like you and me can stand before our holy God with absolutely no fear because Jesus took our sins upon himself on the cross and we are totally forgiven. The great Reformer, Martin Luther, liked to say that God looks at us as if we were as perfect as Jesus. Why? Because Jesus bore our sins on the cross. That's what it means to be justified by Christ's death on the cross.

But some people have raised a huge objection. They say: "That sounds as if at the cross an angry God was beating and bludgeoning to death a poor innocent man. That sounds as if God the Father is so mad at sin that he knocks the you-know-what out of his innocent son. That sounds like child abuse, not divine love and salvation."

My friends, that objection reflects a terrible misunderstanding of the cross. Christian theology teaches that God is Father, Son, and Holy Spirit—three persons in one God. And Christian theology teaches that everything that God does outside God is done by all three persons, Father, Son, and Holy Spirit. That means that God the Father was just as present at the cross as God the Son, Jesus of Nazareth. That means that God the Father suffered just as much at the cross as Jesus did.

The cross brings together two very important things about God. All through the Bible, we learn that God is holy and loving; just and merciful. The biblical God both hates sin and loves sinners. Again and again and again, the Bible tells us how awful sin is and how our holy, righteous God hates sin and punishes it. But the Bible is equally clear that God loves us in spite of our sin and longs to forgive us. The cross brings together God's holiness and God's love in a perfectly wonderful way.

For a holy God, sin is too awful to just be ignored. Think of the terrible evil in our world: Hitler, Stalin, Osama bin Laden, genocide, racism, slavery, murder in our streets, the terrible things that husbands and wives do to each other and their children. It would be a terrible world if these evil things continued forever unpunished.

But our God is also perfect love. God loves even the worst sinners—even Hitler and terrorists.

God longs for every person, no matter how badly they have messed up and violated themselves and others, God longs to forgive every single person—if they will only repent. God is like the father of the prodigal son . God the Father stands ready to run and welcome home every broken daughter and son.

So how does God hold together and reconcile God's searing holiness and God's overflowing love? God does that by dying God-self at the cross. God the incarnate Son takes our sin upon himself, dying physically for our sins. But God the Father is just as present at the cross as God the Son. The Trinity suffers incredible anguish at the cross. The cross is not at all an angry divine Father beating an innocent son to death.

The God who is both holy and loving could have chosen some other way. But God chose to hold together and reconcile God's holiness and God's mercy in this amazing action. Only an infinite God knows how to hold together both divine justice and divine mercy in a perfect way. And our God does that at the cross as God dies in our place.

Notice one more wonderful, crucial thing. God's love triumphs over God's justice. God's final word is unconditional forgiveness to you and me. How do we know that? Because Jesus rose from the dead! If the cross had been the end of Jesus, then God's final word would be that our sin is too awful to be forgiven. But Jesus, who took our deserved punishment on himself at the cross, rose from the dead on Easter morning. Our sins are forgiven, the risen Jesus assures us.

That is what we celebrate in Holy Communion. That is why we run eagerly to the Lord's Supper with arms outstretched, eager to be assured again that we are, right now and forever, totally forgiven and accepted by our holy God because God died for our sins on the cross.

The first thing about Holy Communion then is that it draws us into the astounding benefits that flow to us from the cross of Christ.

II. The Lord's Time Frame

My second point is much briefer.

First Corinthians 11:26 says, "For whenever you eat this bread and drink this cup, you proclaim the Lord's death until he comes."

Notice how the Lord's Supper looks both backwards and forwards.

It looks back to the past—to Christ's death on the cross. As we take the bread and cup, we think about how Christ suffered the agony of Roman crucifixion for us. We rejoice in the fabulous truth that because of the cross we are forgiven. Holy Communion always points us back to that spot outside the city of Jerusalem where, 2,000 years ago, God suffered for our sins.

But the Lord's Supper also points toward the future. Whenever we eat the bread and drink the cup, we proclaim the Lord's death—until he comes! So the Lord's Supper also points forward—to Christ's second coming.

Jesus came as the Messiah proclaiming the gospel of the kingdom. He meant that the messianic time long expected by the Jews was actually beginning. In his preaching and healing, Jesus said, the messianic age of peace and justice was actually taking shape in the present. And Jesus taught his disciples to live according to the standards of the dawning messianic age—empowering the poor, loving their enemies, keeping their marriage vows, abandoning the sinful attitudes and actions between men and women, rich and poor, Jews and Gentiles.

But it was powerfully clear to Jesus and the early church that the messianic kingdom had not come in its fullness. There was still lots of hatred, oppression, and killing around. They knew that sin would completely disappear only at Christ's second coming when he would return to complete his victory over sin, injustice, and even death itself.

Today, the church lives in this interim time—this already/not yet time. The messianic kingdom has already begun. And Christians now seek to live according to the standards of the new messianic kingdom. But that kingdom has not yet fully arrived. Both in the world and even in the church, we see that sin continues its deadly destruction. So we long for the time when Christ will return, complete the kingdom, and make all things new, wiping away all tears from our eyes.

In Holy Communion, we look ahead in hope and longing for that time when each of us will no longer struggle with ongoing temptation and frequent failure. In Holy Communion, we look ahead with joyful expectation to that time when each of us will be fully transformed into the very image of Christ himself and the whole world will be restored to the goodness intended by the Creator.

III. The Lord's Body

This third and final point is a bit longer than the second point about the Lord's time frame, but not as long as the first section on the Lord's cross.

When Jesus broke the bread and gave it to his disciples, he said: "This is my body." What did he mean? The church over the centuries has given different answers. Some have said that the physical body of Jesus is really, literally, present in the bread. Others say that the bread is just a symbol. In what sense, if any, is Jesus Christ truly present in the bread and the cup?

It helps us understand if we remember that Jesus said these words at a Passover celebration with his disciples just before the crucifixion. Every year , the Jews celebrated Passover—to remember the night just before they fled Egypt when all Jewish families sacrificed a lamb, placed the blood on their door, and ate together. That night, God passed over the homes of the people of Israel, not punishing them as God did the Egyptians.

Every year, as Jews remembered and celebrated this crucial moment in their history, they gathered as families and ate unleavened bread just as their ancestors had done hundreds of years before. And the liturgy that the Jews used every year for this annual celebration said the following: "This is the bread of affliction [i.e. unleavened bread] which our ancestors ate when they came from the land of Egypt" (Craig S. Keener, [Grand Rapids: Eerdmans, 1999], 631). Jesus probably said this liturgy with his disciples in that final meal together.

This liturgical statement says literally that this bread they are now eating is the bread the Israelite ancestors had eaten hundreds of years before in Egypt. But nobody thought they meant that literally. They were not saying that bread eaten in the annual Jewish Passover celebration was exactly the same physical bread as that eaten back in Egypt.

Rather, they meant that in some important, powerful, spiritual sense, Jews celebrating the historical event every year were connected to their ancestors at the first Passover. That helps us understand what Jesus meant by saying: "This is my body, this is my blood." I do not think Jesus meant that we are to physically chew his body and drink his blood. What he did mean is that in Holy Communion, we are powerfully participating in Christ himself.

The Lord's Supper is not just a symbolic event. The risen Christ is truly present every time we take communion. The risen Lord who told his disciples after the Resurrection, "Behold, I am with you always, even to the end of the age," is especially present at Holy Communion. He gave us this ritual, this practice, this sacrament, telling us to do it regularly until his return. That means that Christ has chosen to be especially and powerfully present in the bread and the cup. So even though Jesus is not literally physically present in the bread and cup, he is truly, genuinely, in our very midst drawing us to himself, forgiving our sins and transforming us more and more into his very image.

So as we take communion, let's come eagerly, expectantly knowing that the risen Lord is in our very midst with arms wide open, drawing us to himself.

There is one other aspect of the body of Christ that is important in our text that Theresa read from 1 Corinthians 11. Paul begins the passage in verse 17 with a sharp condemnation. He says the Corinthian Christians are coming together for fellowship meals and celebration of the Lord's Supper. But Paul says in verse 20 that they are not really engaging in the Lord's Supper at all. And in verses 27 and 29, Paul says they are sinning against the body and blood of Christ because they do not discern the Lord's body.

Why is Paul so upset and what does he mean? Paul tells us in verses 20–22 that when the Corinthian Christians come together for worship and the Lord's Supper, some Christians have lots of food and feast without sharing their food with other poor Christians in the same Christian congregation who go hungry. Paul says that this failure to share their food with the other members of the church means that they do not discern the body of Christ—i.e., they do not see that every Christian, rich and poor, is a member of Christ's one spiritual body. Paul commands them to eat together, i.e., share their food, when they come together. If they don't do that, they fail to discern the body of Christ, they fail to recognize that every Christian is a part of Christ's one body. Therefore, Christians must share our food and resources wherever there is need in Christ's body.

I think it was way back in 1975 here in Philadelphia that Pope Paul VI said something profound that reflects the teaching of Paul about discerning the body of Christ as we take Holy Communion. The pope said that as long as any Christian anywhere in the world is hungry and in need of help, the eucharistic celebration of all Christians everywhere is imperfect. All Christians in the world are part of Christ's one body. Therefore, if we truly discern the body of Christ at Holy Communion, we will resolve to share our lives and our resources with other Christians in the body of Christ—certainly in our local congregation, but also in our city and around the world. That is why we have a Caring Fund here in our congregation that provides financial assistance to needy members of our congregation. And that's why we participate in Mennonite Central Committee, which helps needy Christians (and others too) in other parts of the world.

So as we take the Lord's Supper, be careful to discern the Lord's body—in two ways. First, although Christ is not present physically, the risen Lord is truly, powerfully, in our midst. And second, as we share the one bread, let's ask Christ to show us how he wants us to share our resources with the other members of Christ's global body.

Today, as we share in Holy Communion, let's reflect on the Lord's cross; let's remember the Lord's time frame that points us to the past and the future; and let's discern the reality of the Lord's body.

The old hymn "Softly and Tenderly" is appropriate for a communion celebration. It wonderfully captures the spirit of the Lord's Supper:

> Softly and tenderly Jesus is calling, calling for you and for me.
>
> See at the portals he's waiting and watching, watching for you and for me.

Come home, come home. You who are weary come
home.

Earnestly, tenderly, Jesus is calling, calling O sinner,
come home.

Communion is for sinners—for broken people struggling to
follow Jesus. Jesus stands at the portals of our hearts, he stands
right here in our midst, with arms wide open, inviting us to turn
to him.

PART FOUR: Finishing Well

Chapter 14: **Living and Dying in the Resurrection**

[A sermon preached on September 30, 2018 at the Landis Homes retirement community in Lititz, Pennsylvania.]

I AM SEVENTY-NINE YEARS old. I'm in pretty good health but there's lots of evidence that my body and my brain are weakening. I'm more forgetful. I need medicine to fix this or that. I usually walk instead of jog. Some of you are younger. But you all know what I am talking about. The truth is, your death, my death, is getting closer and closer.

For many people that is scary. Bertrand Russell was one of the most famous philosophers of the twentieth century. He said that death was no big deal. He said we die, we rot, and then disappear forever. No problem! Many modern intellectuals agree with Russell. But if we exist for a few decades and then disappear forever, what meaning does our short life have?

For 2,000 years, Christians have had a different answer, a wonderful hope. Christians believe that death is not a passage into nothingness. Death is a transition to life eternal in the presence of the risen Jesus.

But can we really believe that promise today in our scientific world? Probably all of us occasionally have doubts.

There's a story told about the great Reformer Martin Luther. Apparently Luther was very ill and everyone thought he would die. But then he recovered. After he was well again, people asked how he felt when he was facing the probability of death. Luther was a good theologian and he said that of course he believed in life eternal. But then Luther added with a slow smile: "Natural reason says that is a big lie." I think we all understand what Luther is saying. We need solid evidence to believe that death does not mark the end of our existence.

St. Paul, however, assures us that in fact because Christ rose from the dead we too shall live. Listen to 1 Corinthians 15:3–8 and 20–23:

> For what I received I passed on to you as of first importance. That Christ died for our sins according to the Scriptures, that he was buried, that he was raised on the third day according to the Scriptures, and that he appeared to Cephas, and then to the Twelve. After that he appeared to more than 500 of the brothers and sisters at the same time, most of whom are still living, though some have fallen asleep. Then he appeared to James, then to all the apostles, and last of all he appeared to me also, as to one abnormally born. . . . Christ has indeed been raised from the dead, the first fruits of those who have fallen asleep. For since death came through a human being, the resurrection of the dead comes also through a human being. For as in Adam all die, so in Christ all will be made alive. But each in this order: Christ the first fruits; then, when he comes, those who belong to him."

It is because Jesus rose from the dead that we can be sure of our living forever with the risen Lord.

I had the privilege of doing my PhD studies with Professor Jaroslav Pelikan. He was probably the most distinguished church historian in the last half of the twentieth century. But he was also a devout Christian. When he died, the bulletin of the Yale history department devoted the whole back page to a description of his many accomplishments. Dr. Pelikan received almost every honor that a scholar could imagine. But at the end of the article, they said that as Dr. Pelikan was dying of cancer, he wrote the last of his many aphorisms: "If Jesus did not rise from the dead, nothing else matters. If Jesus did rise from the dead, nothing else matters." Dr. Pelikan was saying that all of our earthly accomplishments matter nothing at all if we die and disappear forever. He also wanted to say that if we are going to be resurrected and live forever, then all our accomplishments, however wonderful, pale in importance with the fact that we will live eternally with our Lord!

Dr. Pelikan was right. Everything depends on whether Jesus really rose from the dead.

This morning I want to tell you briefly why I am so sure that Jesus of Nazareth was alive on Easter morning. I also want to say why that is so important.

I was trained as an historian. My PhD is in history. I have read many, many books over the last sixty years on the historical evidence for Jesus' resurrection. My conclusion is this: The best historical conclusion is that Jesus' resurrection is a historical fact.

Let me share just four quick reasons for saying that. First, the change in very discouraged disciples. Second, the empty tomb. Third, the fact that the first witnesses were women. And fourth, the very early evidence in 1 Corinthians 15.

Each of those briefly.

A short time after the crucifixion, the disciples announced to a Jerusalem crowd that Jesus had been raised from the dead. Within a few years these same people proceeded to crisscross the eastern part of the Roman empire, braving intense Jewish and pagan persecution and eventually experiencing martyrdom. And it was these very same people who had scattered at Jesus' arrest and fled in despair.

What gave rise to the resurrection faith and the disciples' willingness to risk their lives to spread it? Professor Reginald Fuller, a former professor at Union Theological Seminary, has underlined the fact that this total transformation demands some explanation. He says: "Even the most skeptical historian has to postulate an X to account for the complete change in the behavior of the disciples, who at Jesus' arrest had fled and scattered to their homes, but who in a few weeks were boldly preaching their message to the very people who had sought to crush the movement launched by Jesus" (*The Formation of the Resurrection Narratives* [New York: Macmillan, 1971], 2). The explanation of the people closest to the events of course was that Jesus of Nazareth arose from the tomb and appeared to them over a period of a number of days.

If one rejects the New Testament explanation of the resurrection faith and the transformation it caused in extremely discouraged people, then one is left with the exceedingly difficult task of proposing other grounds adequate to explain this dramatic change. The late Professor Robert Grant of the University of Chicago has said: "The origin of Christianity is almost incomprehensible unless such an event took place"(*Historical Introduction to the New Testament* [New York: Harper, 1963], 376).

Second and very important is the question of the empty tomb. A short time after the crucifixion, Peter claimed that Jesus arose from the dead—and note, he made that claim in Jerusalem. It is exceedingly significant that the controversy over the resurrection, and the rise of the first church, took place precisely in Jerusalem where anybody could have gone to visit the place of burial between supper and bedtime. It was in Jerusalem that thousands became Christians within months of Jesus' death. Obviously it was in the interest of the religious leaders to produce the body of Jesus or give clear evidence of its proper disposal. But the earliest counter argument against the claim that Jesus was alive was the suggestion that the disciples had stolen the body. This was an acknowledgment that the religious leaders could not produce the body.

There have been a number of attempts to explain the empty tomb. The old one of the theft is no longer accepted by anyone. It has been suggested that the Romans or the Jewish leaders removed the body before the women arrived. But if that's what happened, then the Jewish leaders would surely have conducted guided tours to the real burial place as soon as the silly disciples claimed Jesus had risen.

In his discussion of Jesus' resurrection, German Professor Wolfhart Pannenberg says:

> In Jerusalem, the place of Jesus' execution and grave, it was proclaimed not long after his death that he had been raised. The situation demands that within the circle of the first community one had a reliable testimony for the fact that the grave had been found empty. The resurrection kerygma [proclamation] could not have been

> maintained in Jerusalem for a single day, for a single
> hour, if the emptiness of the tomb had not been an es-
> tablished fact for all concerned. (*Jesus: God and Man*
> [Philadelphia: Westminster, 1968], 100)

Since then the Christians and those who disagreed with them both thought that the tomb was empty, it seems very likely that the empty tomb is a historical fact.

Third, the fact that women were the first people to visit the tomb and allegedly see the risen Jesus speaks in favor of the authenticity of the accounts. The late Professor C. F. D. Moule of Cambridge University has pointed out that women were notoriously invalid witnesses according to Jewish principles of evidence. If then the early Christians had fabricated the accounts of the first visit to the tomb and the first meeting with the risen Jesus, they would certainly have claimed that men were the first witnesses. The best explanation for the priority of the women is that it actually happened that way.

Finally we must look at the oldest evidence for the resurrection. In his first letter to the Corinthian church (the date is about 50 to 55 AD), Paul wrote:

> For what I received, I passed on to you as of first im-
> portance: that Christ died for our sins according to the
> Scriptures, that he was buried, then he was raised on the
> third day according to the Scriptures, and that he ap-
> peared to Cephas, and then to the Twelve. After that he
> appeared to more than 500 of the brothers and sisters at
> the same time, though some have fallen asleep. Then he
> appeared to James, then to all the apostles, and last of all
> he appeared to me also, as to one abnormally born.

Paul implies that, if his readers do not believe him, they can check, for many of the eyewitnesses are still around. In fact, the eyewitnesses on both sides saw the rapid spread of Christianity from Jerusalem to Rome.

The most important aspect of this passage, however, is its early date. Many scholars have pointed out that the words used here ("What I received I passed on") are in fact the technical terms used to refer to the careful handing down of oral tradition by Jews. Paul apparently taught this to all the churches. Furthermore Paul says he received it, presumably soon after he became a Christian around 35 AD, just a few years after Jesus' death. That means that this witness to Jesus' resurrection received a fixed form very soon after the actual events (quite possibly before Paul's first post-conversion visit to Jerusalem about 36 AD).

As a historian, I find the evidence surprisingly strong. The most unbiased historical conclusion is that Jesus was probably alive on the third day. The resurrection of Jesus is a historical fact. (For a superb scholarly discussion, see N. T. Wright, *The Resurrection of the Son of God* [Minneapolis: Fortress, 2003].)

Okay, so Jesus really was alive on Easter morning. But why is that important?

First of all, because the resurrection confirms that Jesus is who he said he was. Jesus claimed to be the expected Messiah. He claimed divine authority to forgive sins. At his trial, he said he was the Son of God. The Roman and Jewish authorities crucified him to prove he was wrong. To prove Jesus was a false prophet! If he had stayed dead, that would have been the proper conclusion. But Jesus' resurrection is powerful evidence that the carpenter from Nazareth was indeed the Messiah, the Son of God, true God and true man. That is very important.

But here is what I want to emphasize this morning. Jesus' resurrection shows us both how to live and how to die.

First, Jesus' resurrection shows us how to live. The resurrection confirms that Jesus was not just a good, wise man, but God in the flesh. That means that what Jesus said about how we should live is very important. Jesus taught his disciples to care for the poor; to love their enemies; and to share the gospel with the whole world.

Equally important, it is the resurrected Jesus in our hearts and lives who gives us the power to live what Jesus taught. In Ephesians 1 and 2, Paul says that the same divine power that raised Jesus now lives in us giving us the strength to live like Jesus. The risen Jesus in our hearts gives us the power to live now the way Jesus called his disciples to live.

Now I know you and I cannot do all the things we used to do and still want to do. Our bodies are weaker.

But we can do little things. Praying for our children, grand-children, and great-grandchildren. And praying for peace and justice in our world. We can still share some resources to feed the hungry. We can still vote in a way that empowers poor people, pro-motes peace, opposes racism, and supports truth telling.

It is okay that we cannot do all that we used to do. But God blesses the smaller things we still can do. In fact at the end of 1 Corinthians 15 (Paul's wonderful chapter on the resurrection), Paul says: "Therefore my dear brothers and sisters, . . . always give yourselves fully to the work of the Lord, because you know that your labor in the Lord is not in vain."

Jesus' resurrection shows us that God uses every kind deed or encouraging smile you give to your neighbors at Landis Homes. God uses every prayer, every letter or text to grandchildren. God uses every donation, however small, to empower poor people. God uses every vote to support justice, peace, racial equality, and truth telling. Jesus's resurrection shows us how to live.

And second, thank God, the resurrection also shows us how to die.

I do not mean to pretend that death is a pleasant reality. Of course it is scary to realize that tomorrow or in a few years or a couple of decades our bodies will simply stop working. That is not a pleasant thought. It scares many people. In fact my pastor at Oxford Circle Mennonite Church told me a few years ago that a close friend had told him that many elderly residents at one of the best known Mennonite retirement homes in Pennsylvania were afraid to die.

My brothers and sisters, Christians do not need to be afraid to die. While Jesus was hanging on the cross, he had a conversa-tion with one of the two criminals being crucified with him. Je-sus promised him, "Today you will be with me in paradise." That means that at the moment of death, brothers and sisters in Christ, we move immediately into the presence of the living Jesus. What a wonderful promise from our Lord!

St. Paul told the Corinthians that Jesus is "the first fruits of those who have fallen asleep." Paul meant that what had happened to Jesus at his resurrection will happen to you and me when Christ returns. We will be resurrected bodily! Revelation 21 and 22 portray in powerful pictures that when Christ returns we will live in resurrected bodies in a transformed earth purged of all evil. Death is not the end for Christians. Death is the beginning of a new, even more wonderful existence in the presence of the risen Jesus.

My dad told me that the evening before my mother died, he was sitting beside her holding her hand. Suddenly my mother said, "I think I will go and be with Jesus." Fighting back tears, Dad told her, "Yes, you do that." And the next day mother died resting in the assurance that she was moving to a wonderful future in the presence of her risen Lord.

Sisters and brothers, Jesus rose from the dead. And the resurrection shows us how to live and how to die.

In the words of the Gaithers' wonderful song: "Because he lives, I can face tomorrow, because he lives, all fear is gone. Because I know he holds the future, my life is worth the living just because he lives."